CULTURE AND MANAGEMENT IN JAPAN

CULTURE AND MANAGEMENT IN JAPAN

Shuji Hayashi

translated by
Frank Baldwin

UNIVERSITY OF TOKYO PRESS

Translation of this book was supported in part by a grant from the Ministry of Education, Science and Culture, Japan.

With the exception of the author's name on the jacket and title page, Japanese personal names in this volume are given in the traditional order, with family name first.

Second printing, 1990

ISBN 0–86008–394–2
ISBN 4–13–047040–X

Contents

Preface

This book is a revised version of *Keiei to Bunka* (Management and Culture), which was published in 1984 by Chūō Kōronsha. In order to spare readers many of the original's references to arcane details of Japanese customs and history, I completely rewrote the book for translation into English, and added additional material during the process.

My objective in undertaking this project was twofold: first, to examine how culture affects organizational activity, not only of corporations but of military and educational institutions as well; and second, to look at the relationship between Japan's culture and Japanese-style management.

Most of the numerous volumes that have been written on Japanese management, both works by Japanese and those by Western authors, compare business practices in Japan with those in Europe and North America. This book attempts to contrast Japan with South Korea and the Republic of China (Taiwan), partly by extensive quotation from a trinational survey of businessmen's attitudes in which I participated, and partly by relating my own impressions and conclusions. The conclusions it draws are based both on a survey conducted jointly with academic colleagues in South Korea and Taiwan and on my own impressions gathered in the course of teaching, travel, and study.

Japan, South Korea, and the Republic of China (along with Hong Kong and Singapore) constitute the Confucian cultural sphere, and at the same time the world's most dynamic industrializing region. Confucianism teaches diligence, civility, frugality, and abstinence. Many scholars have noted the similarity between these values and what Max Weber called the Protestant ethic. However, this book attempts to answer two questions: Why did China and Korea, older civilizations than Japan, remain economically stagnant for many centuries? Why was Japan, in contrast, through rapid industrialization and a special kind of business strategy and approach to applied technology, able to join the ranks of the advanced industrial nations?

In Korea, strict adherence to canonical Confucian doctrine blocked modernization. In Japan, however, a blend of Confucian ethics and traditional culture helped Japan to modernize. At the same time, despite the influence of Confucianism and of Western civilization, Japanese never abandoned their distinctive religious and ethical values. Consequently, we have maintained a traditional form of communal solidarity and organizational decision-making. Many of the so-called non-tariff barriers that trade officials and business executives from other countries cite as blocking access to Japanese society and to the Japanese market are merely aspects of Japanese culture. Clarifying this dimension of the problem—not defending Japan's position—is an important personal goal for this book.

I completed the revised manuscript in 1986, which is the Year of the Tiger according to the sexagenary cycle.

Since I was born in 1926, also the Year of the Tiger, under the old way of counting age my life had come full circle. Regarding time as cyclical, an endless revolving flow, is characteristically Oriental, in contrast to the Judeo-Christian view of time as linear. This link between time perception and management methods is one of the important points discussed in the pages that follow.

I wish to thank Dr. Frank Baldwin for translating the revised Japanese manuscript into such lucid and graceful English. I also thank Dr. Kojima Shigeru for contributing his line drawings.

Tokyo, 1988 HAYASHI SHŪJI

CULTURE AND MANAGEMENT IN JAPAN

Chapter One

The Reel of Time

> It was not too surprising for me to discover that cultural time is one of the keys to understanding Japan. To begin with, Japanese time, Zen Buddhism and the concept of MA [space] are all intimately interrelated—relationships which are sometimes difficult for a Westerner to understand. In making this observation, I am not saying understanding the Western mind is any easier for the Japanese. (Edward T. Hall, *The Dance of Life: The Other Dimension of Time*, p. 92)

Edward Hall, a prolific scholar of intercultural communication, has noted that the perception of even an apparently objective concept like time differs from one society to another. Although cultural anthropologists are aware that differences in time perception are a serious barrier to cross-cultural understanding, most laymen, including scholars in the other social and natural sciences and business executives, are not.

Professor Robert Ballon, a management specialist at Sophia University in Tokyo, and well known for his studies of Japanese business, once spoke to a small gathering of company presidents and economists. The topic was "How Do European and American Management Methods Differ?" He diagrammed time orientations on the blackboard in the way illustrated in Figure 1.

Although U.S. managers are situated in and work in the present, in running a business they are always future-oriented, Ballon said. European managers operate in the present, but they always have an eye on the past. U.S. managers esteem vitality, abundance, and mobility; European managers prize experience, necessity, and stability.

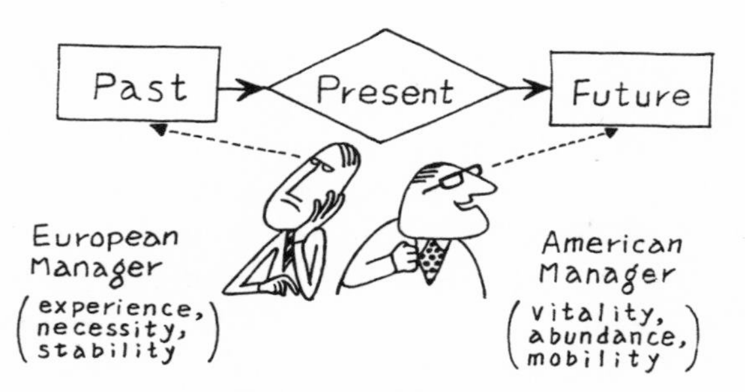

Figure 1. Time Orientations

With the separation of ownership and management in corporations in the United States, professional managers are responsible for corporate decision-making. They look to the future, seek innovation, and aggressively search for new markets. By contrast, in many European enterprises, especially in England and France, the president of a company is the owner or a financier with a banking background. Managers are generally conservative and run the firm with the sole objective of preserving its past glory. These are the major differences in operative motivations between the United States and Europe, according to Professor Ballon.

After this intriguing presentation, a Japanese company president asked which way Japanese managers faced in the diagram. Professor Ballon thought for a while and then replied that Japanese managers are neither future-oriented like their U.S. counterparts nor past-oriented like executives in Europe. They seem to always focus on the here and now—on immediate issues—he said, so they are present-oriented. Ballon thought everyone would agree that two traits of Japanese national character are secularism and realism. Japanese religious sentiment prefers this-worldly benefits, said Ballon. He concluded by saying that many kinds of Japanese behavior are extemporaneous, a "quick fix" for the immediate situation.

The company president responded: "You say Japanese managers are present-oriented, but I doubt it. My work takes me frequently to the United States, and I meet with many managers and chief executive officers. My impression recently is that we are more committed to innovation than they are. Two examples are the use of electronics in the automobile industry and the introduction of robots into small- and medium-sized and traditional industries. Based on my experience, Japanese companies are much more concerned about anticipating change than U.S. firms."

Professor Ballon was not persuaded. Japanese government and industry do not do real long-range analysis and planning, he explained. In the Japanese mode of analysis, even when thinking ahead, there is a strong tendency to posit the future as *an extension of the present*. There are very few speculative leaps into the unknown, attempts to consider it without being bound by current interests and commitments, he said. Thus Ballon concluded that Japanese managers are present-oriented.

It was a fascinating exchange. Unlike a math problem, there is no right and wrong answer. Professor Ballon and the businessman were both partly correct. But this short dialogue showed the vast gap between Westerners and Japanese over the concept of the future.

Cultural Time

We must distinguish between *cultural time* and *physical time*. The latter, based on ideas of physicists about the pattern of the universe, is standardized. Overriding all societal differences, it provides a common framework for measurement and perception. Cultural time, however, is never the same for two societies—or, in some circumstances, for two individuals.

Cultural time perception is classified into two patterns in Figure 2. Pattern A is very similar to Isaac Newton's concept of time as an absolute. It runs from the past to the present, and then toward the future. It is linear, like a straight line on paper. And it is eschatological since time ends with God's judgment, resurrection and immortality.

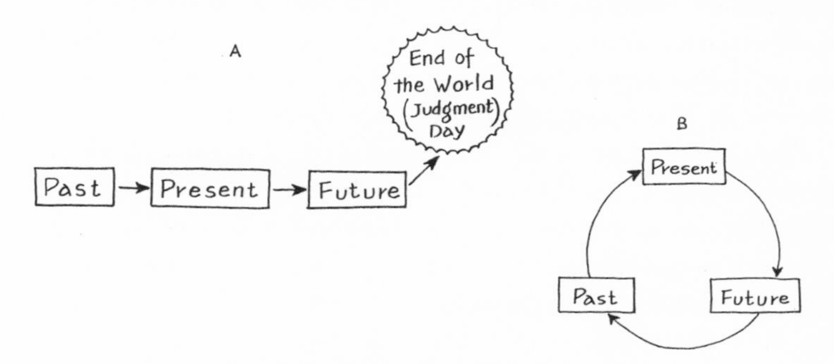

Figure 2. Time Perception Patterns.
A: Linear pattern. B: Cyclic pattern.

Followers of strict monotheistic doctrines like Christianity, Judaism, and Islam generally live by this pattern.

To a devout Christian, for example, cultural time began

when God created the universe and peopled it with Adam and Eve. From the Creation time advances continuously to the Last Judgment. The past is literally a time that has passed and is eternally behind. The souls of the dead have been summoned to God and never return to earth again.

To both Christians and Muslims, human beings in this world live in awe of an absolute God's judgment on the final day. I call this a linear time perception pattern.

Pattern B, with its circular, perpetual-movement character, I call a cyclic or circular time perception pattern. Followers of polytheistic religions like Hinduism and Buddhism live by this cultural time. Metempsychosis holds that when human beings die, the spirit/soul is reborn in another body, either human or animal. Transmigration continuously recurs in an eternal ring.

Mishima Yukio's final work, the tetralogy *The Sea of Fertility*, beautifully describes the world as a phantastic stage where human beings are reincarnated. To Western readers and to many Japanese today as well, it is a mysterious, eerie saga. The tetralogy seems to use the structure of Noh, the traditional musical-dance drama. Most Noh main stages are divided into a front half and a rear stage. The plays have a leading character (*shite*) who changes his appearance or even becomes an entirely different person, and a subordinate character (*waki*) who watches the *shite* as an observer and moves around the stage.

In *The Sea of Fertility*, a man named Honda appears in all four books in a subordinate role, that of the *waki*. The leading character is reborn many times, changes his appearance, and appears on the Noh stage of contemporary life. Noh dramas are closely linked to the spiritual world of Japanese, and all plays have this cyclic time pattern. The day Mishima completed the tetralogy, he committed ritual suicide, in a dramatic example of art and life coming full circle.

Although Christians regard suicide as a sin, Japanese have not thought of death as a final parting from this world, but traditionally have seen it as the occasion for the rebirth of the soul. Many frequently used expressions attest to the ubiquity of this attitude. For example: "Seven reincarnations are insufficient to repay obligations to one's master." Another: "The karma of previous existence determines the circumstances of this life." Cultural time pattern B underlies Buddhism, which has strongly influenced Japanese life.

Followers of Christianity and Islam are usually taught that to prepare for the final day of judgment, human beings must uphold their faith, do good deeds, and accumulate religious grace. Standard Buddhist teaching, however, is that one who follows Buddha's teachings and does good deeds will be born into a good life at the time of reincarnation. Popular Buddhist literature like the *Birth Stories* (*Jātaka*) is full of stories about transmigrations of the soul.

First introduced to Japan from Korea in the mid–sixth century, Buddhist doctrine subsequently became a major spiritual force. Yet it never had the all-encompassing success that Christianity achieved in Europe, where it became *the* faith. For that reason, also, contemporary Japanese do not accept completely a cultural time pattern of reincarnation like that of Indian Hinduism or Tibetan Buddhism. The average Japanese follows neither a linear model nor a pure cyclic model that expects an afterlife. As Professor Ballon said, the outlook is more secular and realistic.

Makimono Time

Figure 3 is an attempt to portray Japanese cultural time. This chart is taken from Tanabe Hajime's (1885–1962) *Historical Reality*. Professor Tanabe, who taught at Kyoto University, combined a thorough knowledge of Western philosophy with erudite scholarship on Oriental thought. According to Tanabe, the structure of historical time (cultural time indigenous to Japanese, in my terminology) is not linear like physical time but resembles an unfurling spiral.

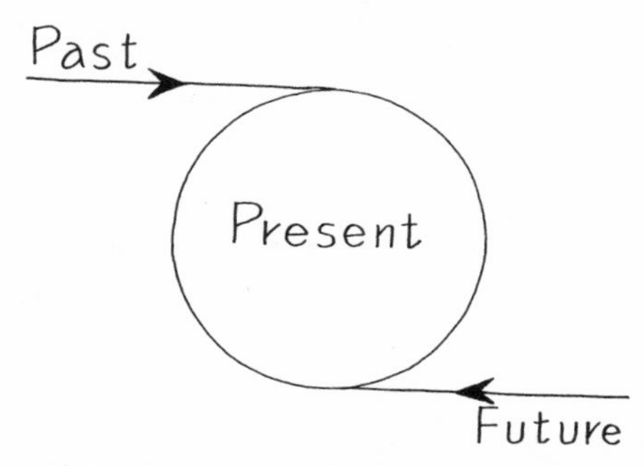

Figure 3. Makimono Time Perception Pattern

I call the pattern illustrated in Figure 3 a makimono time perception pattern, after the makimono, a picture story or writing mounted on paper and usually rolled into a scroll.

The symbolic significance of these patterns of time perception is far-reaching. In Western linear time, the past can be thought of as over and done with, something that has disappeared forever to a far-off place beyond the reach of contemporary human beings; it does not recur. Likewise, the future is off in the distance ahead, beyond our knowledge and grasp.

But in the makimono time pattern, the past has not exited into eternity with the finality of a slammed door; it still exists in the present. In the religious and humanistic gestalt of the average Japanese, the spirits or souls (*sorei*) of dead ancestors return at least once a year. On *bon*, the midsummer Buddhist festival of the dead, the spirits visit descendants' families, share a meal, and form a happy household again. The *sorei* are always near and protect their descendants from calamities. Japanese think of the past as linked to and existing in the present. By the same token, they do not like to think of the future as totally beyond the reach of contemporary human knowledge and will. Although believers in a monotheistic god avow that the future is in His hands, the average Japanese thinks the future can be pulled towards the present and brought under control by human effort. The future is like a kite flying in the distant sky that can be reeled back to earth.

Professor Ballon pointed this out when he said Japanese try to posit the future as an extension of the present. Cultural anthropologists in Japan attribute the doting protectiveness adults lavish on children in Japan to a subconscious feeling that children are our ancestors reincarnate.

In Japanese cultural time the past flows continuously toward the present, and the future is also firmly linked to the present. In philosophical terms, we might say the past and the future simultaneously exist *in the present*. To symbolize this notion in Figure 3, both the past and the future are headed toward the present where they rendezvous, like two streams converging from opposite directions. In a Western book or personal letter, the writer often treats the past, present, and future separately; each time period is given a different chapter or paragraph. But in old Japanese books and letters, events in the past, descriptions of the contemporary scene, and speculations about what would probably happen in the future were often depicted in one long, continuous makimono.

Many first-time visitors to Japan—Westerners in particular but Asians too—are surprised to see the past side by side with the present. Japanese are unaware of this temporal juxtaposition and take it for granted. Discovering that both traditional culture and the latest industrial innovations are part of everyday life, visitors often remark that in Japan the past and future peacefully coexist. The past and future rush toward a moment in physical time—

the present—where they swirl together like a benign whirlwind. Non-Japanese sense this confluence.

I once accompanied an industrial survey team from the People's Republic of China (PRC) on a visit to a steel plant. They were startled to see a tiny Shinto shrine carefully fastened to the world's largest and newest cupola, a furnace for melting metals. The group wondered why Japanese workers had placed a primitive animistic symbol on this product of high technology. The Chinese dignitaries, materialists all, could not fathom the combination. I asked the plant supervisor, "What god does that shrine honor?" He explained as follows.

"There was a shrine here to a Shinto deity who has protected this spot since ancient times. We tore it down to build the cupola, but we have kept the god here. We pray to it every day before we start working, to safeguard the unit. Thanks to it, we haven't had a single accident since the cupola began operating."

Although Japanese are generally considered Buddhists, their religious sentiments include a deeply rooted animistic faith in native gods who predate Buddhism. These beliefs are still strong today. Spirit-like beings—the *sorei* and the cupola's protective deity—are usually called *kami* or *kamisama*. (These terms are often translated as "god" or "deities," but the numerous *kamisama* should not be confused with the deities of Greek mythology or the absolute god of a monotheistic religion.)

Japan is probably the only advanced industrial country whose population still embraces such primitive religious notions. Most civilized peoples, even if at one stage they practiced an animistic religion, discard it in favor of a "higher" world religion like Christianity, Islam, or Buddhism. Although Buddhism and Christianity spread to Japan, the populace was not converted to one faith to the exclusion of other beliefs. A subtle fusion, a détente, was worked out between the new religions and belief in *kami*. In Japan the past is still a vibrant force in the present; a grasp of this dynamic is crucial to understanding Japanese-style management and organizational dynamics.

I have escorted many foreign scholars around Kyoto. Even those with little interest in the famous Buddhist temples and monasteries were impressed by the Fushimi Inari Shrine in the ancient capital's southern suburb. Although the Chinese-red wooden building dates from the late fifteenth century, it has been well maintained and looks as if it were built yesterday. Inari, the shrine deity, was originally associated with rice agriculture. At some point it was adopted as a guardian deity by the Shingon sect of Buddhism, and it has survived to the present. Each year the Fushimi Inari Shrine ranks first or second nationwide in number of visitors. The mountain behind the main shrine building is covered with brilliant Chinese-red torii, the stylized Shinto gateway, inscribed with the names of contributors from all over Japan. The path from the entrance to the shrine's approach road to the top of the mountain is packed with tens of thousands of torii. Worshippers pass through this vermilion tunnel to reach the inner shrine. Beside the road like scattered leaves are small subordinate shrines, each sparkling brightly with a votive candle. Many worshippers pause in prayer. At this sight, the typical comment of foreign friends is: "I have heard that Japanese are not religious, but that is clearly not true. The ancient folkways still have meaning."

Animism in South Korea

Are ancient folk beliefs also still strong in the Republic of Korea? The question is relevant because of geographical propinquity and the peninsula's cultural affinity with Japan.

Although animistic and other old folkways still have many followers in some rural areas of South Korea, such beliefs are officially regarded as scurrilous paganism. Educated Koreans call them superstition, and animism is not openly practiced.

The Yi dynasty (1392–1910) made Confucianism a state religion and suppressed folk beliefs. The literati also attacked Buddhism, which had been a force on the peninsula for a millennium. (In Japan, also, the Tokugawa shogunate [1600–1867] made Confucian values the core of an orthodox education. Nevertheless, neither Shintoism nor Buddhism was suppressed.) A humanistic philosophy, Confucian rationalism rigorously opposed popular religion. According to the *Analects*, "The Master did not talk about weird things, physical exploits, disorders and spirits." Confucianism denied the existence of gods and supernatural phenomena caused by spirits; it affirmed a faith in man. Under its pervasive sway, animistic deities and Buddhist bodhisattvas were purged from Korean society.

The ruling stratum of Korea until the nineteenth century, the *yangban* class, led the attack on folk religion as the self-conscious guardians of the rationalist Confucian legacy from China. Today, South Korean intellectuals, spiritual heirs to the *yangban*, speak of animism with disgust and usually deny it still exists. The most they will concede is that "it may be practiced secretly by uneducated peasants in some farm villages."

As we have seen, in Japan the opposite is true. Factories have small animistic shrines with a protective deity who watches over the equipment and facilities. On ceremonial days, company presidents preside over ceremonies at the bright red torii of Inari shrines on the roofs of high-rise office buildings. There are midday processions down the busiest city streets in religious rites to honor ancient gods.

Korean and Japanese attitudes toward cultural borrowing also differ radically. Koreans are not readily inclined to accept exogenous culture. Yet once they have decided to do so, there is a tendency to discard the old culture—elements worthy of retention as well as those that have outlived their usefulness. The baby is thrown out with the bath water. Japanese are receptive to new and exogenous culture, which they blend harmoniously with their own historical legacy. We never cast off tradition, either the valuable or the worthless; our society is a museum of anachronisms. We prefer to modernize the past and preserve it for the future.

Politics is a good example. The imperial institution dates from at least the sixth century; a parliamentary system modeled on Western democracy was added in the nineteenth century. The emperor functioned simultaneously as the patriarch of an indigenous animistic faith and as the head of state of a Western-style democracy. Making dissimilar forms work together is the genius of Japanese cultural accretion. No society elsewhere in Asia or in Africa has so successfully meshed the new and the old.

Japanese-style management is also a syncretic blend, thanks to the cultural time pattern in which the past and the future meet, simultaneously and compatibly, in the present. The young man who enjoys carrying a portable Shinto shrine—dedicated to an obscure god whose name he may not even know—through the streets is the same junior executive who is fascinated by the newest computer or industrial innovation. One of his personae has roots in the ancient past; the other has a vision of the future.

Lacquerware and Makimono Time

This makimono syndrome is manifested in our products. Wooden lacquerware has long been recognized as a beautiful Japanese craft. The word *japan* in English means a lacquer or varnish with a hard, glossy finish, and objects decorated in this Japanese style. The traditional method of making lacquerware entails hard, demeaning labor. It takes many years to become a master craftsman; during the long apprenticeship the worker's skin is poisoned by the lacquer, which is the sap of the *urushi*. Although workers gradually develop an immunity to the lacquer, their hands are stained black, as if they have been badly burned in a fire. Wajima, in Ishikawa Prefecture at the tip of the Noto Peninsula on the Japan Sea, is known for its outstanding lacquerware. To prevent minute particles of dust from ruining the finish, when it is applied, artisans work on small boats offshore even in the dead of winter, braving the bitter cold from the continent. The process takes many days.

If lacquerware admirers knew how the utensils were made, they might not enjoy their beauty. Humanistic concern would demand safer materials. The craft would die out and Wajima's marvelous lacquerware would be found only in museum showcases, silent testimony to the arduous labor of master workmen of the past.

But fear not. Japanese artisans, true to their makimono time culture, have found a way to continue the craft. Groups of small, local makers, the mainstay of the industry, have begun to use industrial robots. Workers are no longer in danger of poisoning; the lacquering is done 24 hours a day in dust-free rooms. The finish is just as beautiful as ever. A traditional craft and state-of-the-art technology have been successfully combined. The woodcarving industry is another example. In Takato, Nagano Prefecture, long a center of wood craft, companies are using laser beams to do precision carving of art objects.

The individuals who adopted this advanced technology were not executives in large corporations in the high-tech sectors; they were operators of small businesses in the most conservative fields. Japanese industrialists always bring *something really old and something futuristic together in the present.* The makimono cultural time pattern sets the stage for unique encounters of a profitable kind between the past and the future.

Western workers have often bitterly resisted modern technology. During the Industrial Revolution the Luddite movement in England destroyed new machines, and in recent years some British labor unions have opposed the use of robots. In 1987, about 5,500 production workers went on strike against the introduction of computerized technology by publisher Rupert Murdoch. The dispute led to mass firings, violence, and suspected arson. Nothing like this has happened in Japan, although there has been some obstructionism by workers influenced by Western labor-movement ideology. Many factors may be hypothesized to account for why traditional industries and the work· force in Japan have not opposed new machinery, but I think the cultural explanation is persuasive.

Word Processing and Language

The Japanese-language word processor, which made its debut in the early 1980s, is another case of technology rescuing tradition. Though word processors were initially quite expensive, the price dropped sharply, and the product has been widely adopted. With the word processor, for the first time Japanese had a practical mixed-script typewriter. Written Japanese consists of ideographs—Chinese characters (*kanji*)—that express meaning, and two phonetic syllabaries, *hiragana* and *katakana*, that express sound. Characters were introduced from China in the fifth century; though written exactly as on the continent, they were pronounced differently in Japan. The two script systems were devised in Japan a few centuries later. Each Japanese syllabary (*kana*) has about 50 symbols, whereas there are several thousand characters in regular use. Thus, a Japanese typewriter could only use *kana*. The disadvantage of *kanji* is the enormous intellectual labor of learning them; their redeeming virtue is that once they have been memorized, words are like pictures and can be read very quickly. Skilled postal clerks in Japan are said to sort mail three times as fast as their U.S. counterparts because ideographs can be scanned so rapidly. The mixed-script systems invented by Japanese and Koreans combine ideographs and phonetic symbols, but *kanji* make them virtually impossible to type.

In recent years, owing to changes in the educational system, an increasing number of young Japanese (and South Koreans) have difficulty recalling and writing *kanji*, although they can recognize them for reading purposes. It is much easier to read a text with a moderate number of characters than one written all in *kana*. However, many young people are able to use more *kanji* when working with word processors than when they write by hand. Similarly, until the 1970s, the address labels on direct-mail postal matter and station names on Japanese National Railways' computerized tickets were printed in *kana*. Now characters are used, and both are much easier to read.

During the Allied Occupation of Japan (1945–52) a serious attempt was made to reform Japanese into a phonetic language. Proponents called for a total shift to Roman letters or at least the abolition of *kanji* and the use of *kana* symbols only. Although Occupation policy favored language reform, a more important reason was that many Japanese were apprehensive about the limitations of a mixed-script language for data processing. They reasoned that when computers came into widespread use and communications were automated, it would be impossible to process a mixed script with such complex ideographics. These reformers agreed that *kanji* should be abolished and phonetic *kana* used exclusively. At the time I thought *kanji* would gradually be eliminated and eventually the language would be written completely in *kana*. Such a shift seemed inevitable, a transformation whose time had come.

These expectations were brilliantly betrayed. The development of microchips led to word processors that can handle thousands of *kanji* and compound words made of two or more characters, a feat that defied the typewriter. Now anyone can easily type Japanese. Just as traditional lacquerware production received an eleventh-hour reprieve from robotics, the apparently doomed mixed-script writing system was saved by the semiconductor. On the brink of extinction, both reached into the future and survived.

Likewise, in the political sphere, Japan infused the ancient imperial institution with a new dynamism by adopting Western parliamentary democracy. (However, the superimposition of political parties on a culture still based on the village style of organization means that while ruling and opposition parties operate in principle as Western parties do, in practice the ruling party leaders vie for position much as village elders fight over leadership.)

The Future as Past

In *The Devil's Dictionary*, Ambrose Gwinnett Bierce called the present "that part of eternity dividing the domain of disappointment from the realm of hope." A Japanese definition would say: "The present is a temporal period that links the region of the past with the world of the future." Rather than a dividing point, Japanese have always made the present a go-between introducing the past to the future.

The disagreement between Professor Ballon and the Japanese executive over whether U.S. or Japanese managers are more future-oriented was predictable. Professor Ballon, a Westerner and a Christian, uses a linear time perception pattern. The Japanese company president functions on a circular time perception pattern. The two men live in different cultural time-frames and have contradictory images of the future; neither was aware of the gap in basic assumptions.

The Japanese think and act according to a cultural time structurally different from other societies. We are not (*pace* Professor Ballon) simply present-minded. Our perspective of "now" is always affected by both the bygone and the imminent. That is why the company president insisted that Japanese managers sedulously look ahead.

Such clashes, frequent among people from different cultures, are one of the challenges in operating a multinational corporation or a joint venture. Working together on strategic planning, for example, could be quite difficult for Japanese and American executives because of their disparate images of the future.

Are there people with a linear cultural time perception who nonetheless lack interest in the past or future and live exclusively in the present? The desert nomads of the Middle East are a classic example. The people of Greece also have a present-oriented time culture. A Greek government pamphlet, in a description of the national temperament, says Greeks are a lighthearted, cheerful people fond of relaxing and fun, who want to avoid trouble as much as possible. According to the pamphlet, when something unpleasant occurs, Greeks immediately suggest that it be dealt with the following day, and then secretly hope the next day will never come. In disputation, most Greeks seem to enjoy exploring the complex aspects of a problem rather than rapidly reaching a conclusion, the account says. Travelers are assured that when lost or in need of assistance, villagers will drop what they are doing and help them. The pamphlet warns that time is not especially meaningful along the Mediterranean coast. Although appointments and schedules are made, there is no stringent sense of obligation to observe them.

This is a textbook description of a "now" culture with a linear time perception. Easygoing people, Greeks do not brood about the past and prefer not to think about the future. They live wholeheartedly in the "now." Someone trying to get a firm commitment from a Greek is often told "Tomorrow," but the appointment may not be kept the next day.

Many Japanese business people have similar experiences with Arabs. When an executive from Tokyo tries to nail down an appointment or arrangement for the next day, the standard response is "If Allah permits." The attitude is, "We don't know what tomorrow might bring." Arabs are not fastidious about engagements scheduled a day in advance, Japanese executives complain. A reluctance to make commitments can be a form of evasiveness, but more often it illustrates a contrast in time culture. Japanese think that we ourselves determine tomorrow today; Arabs believe that tomorrow is at the disposal of an absolute god, not of mere mortals.

Corporate managers cannot neglect strategic planning; vague statements like "Nobody knows what the future will bring" are no excuse for inaction. Nomads and desert peoples, who pay less heed to the past or future and live boldly in the present, find it extremely difficult to adapt to modern management techniques. By contrast, Japanese and Americans, although they have different cultural time patterns, are always thinking ahead to what the future will be like or are applying scientific and technical breakthroughs to production and goods. This temperament has enabled both peoples to become, by dint of their own efforts, major industrial powers.

A comparison of Japanese, Taiwanese, and South Korean management methods would help to explain how these East Asian tigers have made the Pacific Rim a prosperous lair. Although I have discussed cultural time perceptions and attitudes toward the future with many Taiwanese and Korean entrepreneurs and management experts, unfortunately I cannot yet offer a trilateral hypothesis. I can say with certainty, however, that Chinese and Korean time cultures differ from those described above, including the Japanese. Although both countries share with Japan a similar East Asian historical experience, one reason for their much later industrialization was that Chinese and Koreans lacked a future-oriented time culture. Indians (and Tibetans), with their metempsychosical image of the future, also lagged far behind in industrialization.

Americans tend to see the future as separate from the past or present, a radically different dimension. Japanese regard it as an extension of the past or present, a further refinement of what has already existed. This dissimilarity has profound consequences. Westerners are called "creative" and Japanese are labelled "improvers," yet both sets of skills basically stem from subconscious cultural differences.

Creativity Versus Refinement

Japanese are widely criticized for lacking creativity and being incorrigible imitators of foreign products. The standard apologia has been that Japan was a developing country and tried to catch up quickly by copying what Westerners had created. I think national character is a better explanation. To say that we are talented at *refining* things is more accurate. In the philosophic dichotomy between the Ideal and the Real, Japanese favor the latter. Instead of a soaring flight of inventiveness that results in something totally new, our forte is a more pedestrian approach: the steady refinement of extant objects. Japanese are always implementing variations; minor changes will do.

Even when a simple imitation of a product would suffice, a Japanese is not satisfied with just that. Whether the original is foreign-made or domestically produced, there is a determination to add a new twist that improves the item or modifies its purpose. A mere imitator should be content if his product is as good, or almost as good, as the model. Over the centuries, with great zest, Japanese have always been improvers or modifiers of products. This trait is less a sign of business zeal than the result of technocratic perfectionism.

Modern military science in Japan dates from the mid-sixteenth century, when Portuguese firearms were first introduced. Within a year Japanese had produced two guns based on the Portuguese models; within ten years domestic producers not only filled local demand but were exporting weapons, superior to the original prototypes, to nearby countries. Japanese gun makers reportedly used better iron, and the barrels withstood many discharges without shattering. Today, the domestically produced tanks of the Ground Self-Defense Forces have sophisticated features second to none. Portuguese playing cards brought to Japan in the sixteenth century were quickly imitated. But a better-quality paper was used and other changes were made to suit Japanese preferences. Today, state-of-the-art materials and techniques are used to produce, for example, the new currency notes introduced in 1984.

After World War II, Japanese first imitated and then mass-produced many foreign products: German cameras, Swiss watches, and U.S. automobiles. In each case, our companies were clearly more concerned with refining the original product than with just turning out an imitation, and this is still true. A Japanese plastics expert, Yuasa Sadao, who examined an artificial heart developed at the University of Utah, was quoted by the science journal *Ka-*

gaku Asahi as saying, "I could easily improve this and make a more sophisticated version." Original products are constantly refined in Japanese hands. Where does this zeal for innovation come from? I attribute it to the Japanese cultural time pattern—the concern to preserve the old and infuse it with a new vitality as a gift to posterity.

In the late 1940s, the American physicist William Shockley invented the transistor, for which he was awarded the Nobel Prize in physics in 1956. In the late 1950s transistors began to replace vacuum tubes. Americans immediately applied transistors to space exploration, military communications, and weapons. Having a future orientation based on linear time, they naturally thought of transistors in terms of applications that would make it easier to leave the earth, explore the solar system, and reach out to a new universe.

The Japanese, with their makimono time pattern and tinkering approach, saw different applications for the transistor: they thought in terms of miniaturizing and reducing the weight of the radio, for example, which everyone needs and uses, and making it portable—literally put it into people's hands. This required low-cost, large-scale production of highly reliable transistors. Japanese industry was able to do this, and the rest is history: the first transistor radios came on the market in 1954, and in 1965 Sony marketed the first transistorized television sets. While Americans treated the transistor as a precious, expensive item and used it to unravel the mysteries of space, we made it a cheap, mass-produced component and improved household appliances. The conceptual applications were totally different. I make no value judgment on these approaches, but the result was that Japanese companies captured the world electronics market.

This kind of Japanese response to scientific breakthroughs is a major cause of Tokyo's trade friction with the United States and Europe. With both transistors and integrated circuits, in the pre-mass-production stage the defect rate and cost were high. This is permissible when manufacturers produce only for new high-tech fields like space or sophisticated weapons systems, as the Americans did. However, if makers apply transistors or semiconductors to products like radios, as the Japanese did, the components must be reliable and cheap. Thus Western manufacturers complain that "the Japanese mass-produce all kinds of quality merchandise and then the prices drop." The examples in consumer goods are legion. With German cameras, Swiss watches and French haute couture, generally Western manufacturers targeted an affluent stratum of the market and turned out, under craft-like conditions, a limited volume. Japanese makers mass-produced these products for the average consumer.

Nurtured in a makimono cultural time that extends back to the distant past, we are better at modifying existing products than at creating original ones. This has become a national forte. The charge that Japanese are imitative misses the point: our Weltanschauung esteems improvement and refinement.

Westerners have long had a special flair for challenging the unknown. From the fifteenth century, Europeans, dissatisfied with their "cramped" territory, began to explore dangerous sea routes and claim new territory. In America, settlers braved danger and adversity to spread across the continent until the frontier ended at the Pacific Ocean. Now Americans are passionately engaged in space exploration, a spinout from the earth to the cosmos. With few exceptions, Japanese were content on their narrow archipelago until the mid-nineteenth century, when the Western powers forced the doors open to international contact. Generally speaking, we eschewed grand adventures, remained at home in familiar environs, and created a culture not by imitation but through incremental improvements.

Time culture is closely linked to the language, literature, and religion of each cultural sphere. If linear time goes with Christianity and Islam and cyclic time with Hinduism and Buddhism, then makimono time must be associated with the unique religious outlook of Japanese, *Nihonkyō* (Japanism), which, along with Buddhism and Confucianism, has been called a basic thought or belief system of the Japanese people. (The term was popularized by the writer "Isaiah Ben-Dasan," a self-described rabbi and author of the 1970 bestseller *The Japanese and the Jews*. "Isaiah Ben-Dasan" is widely thought to be the essayist and social critic Yamamoto Shichihei.) Japan's industry, corporations, and domestic market, which are all affected by makimono time and *Nihonkyō*, have special characteristics, some of which are strengths and others weaknesses.

The adventuresome, revolutionary mind-set of Westerners, especially of Americans, always seeks new worlds to conquer. Risk-taking and discovery are supreme values. Christians are instinctually aware that with this kind of progress, mankind eventually must face God's judgment because of the hubris of science and technology. In other words, a linear time perception assumes that humankind's inevitable fate is death.

The Japanese way of thinking favors the gradual, mundane, and peaceful. Rooted in human activities, this approach inspires no brilliant breakthroughs or heroic sagas. But neither does it lead to a future that terminates in cataclysm. People with a cyclic or makimono time perception are exempt from Promethean pride, as well as from the notion of sin. (Sin is a feature of monotheism; the concept does not exist in polytheism or ancestor worship.)

Readers with a linear time perception may regard statements that the Japanese are deficient in creativity or are only capable of refining things as a damning indictment. But if mankind's survival is important, this is a healthy, moderate approach. In makimono time, as the thread of the past is slowly let out and the line to the future is hauled in, the present advances gradually like a rolling ball of yarn. Unlike the essentially stagnant time of linear and cyclic patterns, the Japanese "now" is in motion toward tomorrow, next year, the next decade.

Japan's industrial economy, which is undergirded by a distinctive view of the present and future, has a managerial perspective and approach to technology found nowhere else in the world. These have created a manufacturing sector that contributes to the welfare of humanity. Although Japanese companies are less zealous in coming up with original technology and developing new fields, they constantly improve existing products and make them available to tens of millions of people. This manufacturing style should not be confused with copying or turning out me-too products.

Japanese corporate behavior, however, given the realities of the world economy, often causes angry reactions abroad when Japan-made products capture markets. Japanese firms must in some way pay compensation, perhaps by bearing part of the costs incurred by the original inventors of the technologies being exploited. In the field of small computers, for example, Japanese companies have been very skillful at producing and selling equipment compatible with U.S. products. In March 1983, Xerox sued Japan's NEC Corporation for infringement of patents because NEC, which refused to pay compensation, began to sell Xerox-compatible products. The U.S. firm argued, reasonably enough, that NEC's free ride—letting another company bear all the development costs and then jumping into the market to rake off the profits—was unfair.

American science and basic research open the door to the future; Japan's manufacturing industry skillfully refines what others create. These are complementary and compatible strengths.

Language and Time

Language is a basic element of culture, and one which defines how time is experienced.

When I began to study English, the first thing that struck me as strange was the distinction made between the past tense and the present perfect tense. An action that is completely over is in the past tense; an action that although over has an ongoing effect or after-image is in the present perfect. In modern Japanese these two are not differentiated.

In the Japanese way of thinking, originally there was no need to distinguish the two. We implicitly perceive nearly all past phenomena as present-perfect events. To us, the past is not over and done with but part of the here and now. The statement "I was assisted by him" means "At a certain time in the past he helped me" and "I am still indebted to him for that aid." The act is not consigned to a category called "finished"; it rolls on in the present like an eternal echo. The past is experienced in the present perfect.

When a Japanese receives some kindness from another person, he says *arigatō* (thank you). Another oft-used phrase is *sumimasen.* A literal translation is "not yet finished," from the verb *sumu* (to end, terminate, be concluded) and the negative inflection. The meaning is "I am indebted to you for a kindness I have not returned." Most foreigners just starting to study the language say *arigatō,* but those who are sensitive to Japanese feelings—the affective dimension—use *sumimasen.* The latter is the appropriate word because it conveys a very pleasing refined gratitude.

Japanese work hard to preserve the momentum of beneficial personal ties or acts. In the West, when a visitor is feted at a welcome banquet, if at all possible the recipient gives a return affair for the host. This quick symbolic repayment stems from a rational concern that neither party be indebted to the other. That has not been the custom in

Japan. On the contrary, the newer the acquaintance, the less likelihood of a prompt repayment. To requite an obligation immediately is regarded as unfriendly, a ploy to avoid further involvement. The correct response is for the honored person to simply say *sumimasen*: "I am in your debt, the beneficiary of your kindness." Like certain wines, the debt of gratitude should be allowed to age, because it improves the relationship. This delayed reciprocity sustains the friendship of the original event into the present and future. However, this behavior is probably limited to situations when we know that the other party functions under the same cultural time. Outsiders to the culture may have a very different experience.

Americans sometimes seem to regard the ability to break an intense relationship as a manly virtue. The scene in Westerns where the hero says "Goodbye" and rides off gallantly into the sunset without a backward glance has stirred audiences for films from *Shane* to *Pale Rider*. Historically, the Japanese have been a sedentary farming people who could not imagine living somewhere cut off from their ancestors. Separation is traumatic. The Western gunslinger's stoic departure suggests that he is a descendant of a hunting or nomadic people.

Scenes of parting or suicide by harakiri in Japanese dramas are usually slow and prolonged. A group of visiting South Korean college students reported they were surprised at how Kabuki death scenes are stretched out. In Korean dramas these events are much briefer, they said. I think this is because Koreans come from a northern nomadic stock accustomed to moving on.

The standard Japanese equivalent for "Goodbye" is *sayōnara*, but the latter word has a different nuance, closer to "Till we meet again." We think of our bodies as somehow tied to our ancestors; the idea of permanent separation is painful. Japanese vaguely believe that human beings will meet again at some point in the eternity of time.

In an essay entitled "Time in the Japanese Novel," Barbara Yoshida-Craft, a German-born specialist on Japanese literature, quotes from several prominent writers to describe the eddy of events in fiction. "It is the exception for a story to be written exclusively in the past tense. In a sentence describing facts in the past, often the writer changes to the present tense." She adds, "The present in the Japanese language is distinct from the past and the future, but not completely cut off from either. Rather, it is one point of contact in a temporal experience. . . . In a sense, there is an invisible point where past and future meet." She concludes that "what we usually call a sense of time—how it is felt and divided into units—is different in Japanese and German." Her point is not that Japanese writers mix the past and present. She is warning Western readers not to conclude that in Japanese literature (or management methods) the time frame is weak or the overall structure poorly done.

Forecasting

Some years ago, as a member of the Ministry of Transport's advisory council on transportation policy, I participated in a project to predict the demand for freight transport until 1990. Looking at the period from 1981 to 1990, the council estimated that freight volume would increase for trucks, coastal shipping, and airplanes. It was obvious to everyone that railway freight shipments would decrease. Nevertheless, officials of the ministry and the Japanese National Railways (JNR)[1] published an estimate that showed railway freight volume as virtually unchanged until 1990.

[1] The JNR in 1987 was privatized in the form of five regional companies, which are collectively known as the JR (Japan Railways).

Table 1. Estimated domestic freight volume, 1981–1990
(unit: 10 billion ton-km)

	1973	1979	1990 (estimate)
Marine transportation	207.7	225.8	410–450
Truck	141.0	172.9	230–260
Railway	58.3	43.1	34– 43
Total	407.2	442.1	690–740

Source: Ministry of Transport statistics.

Why was this done? No matter how officials juggled the figures, it was impossible to forecast an increase in railway freight tonnage. Yet to declare that volume would decline sharply would have been a clear admission of impending desuetude and fiscal crisis for the system. Instead, they said that volume would change very little in the years ahead. To honestly predict a reduction would have been tantamount to saying to JNR freight employees, "The work you are doing will decrease this much within a decade." Rail officials declined to publish an objective forecast out of sympathy for the affected personnel.

Professor Ballon's comment is apt for this JNR estimate: In thinking about the future, Japanese do not seem able to free themselves from the present and objectively look at a time ahead. And I agree that neither the Japanese government nor corporations seem capable of long-range analysis and planning. Regarding high technology, Japan is enthusiastic about short-term planning—a time frame where the payoff is near at hand—but neither the government nor entrepreneurs will spend money on, or even show much interest in, the kind of long-term planning that inspires people to dream of noble deeds. This has been the outlook of Japanese since ancient times. To put the best light on it, we have always been a very realistic, mundane people.

Westerners seem to have a farsighted perspective in planning a project. Construction of a large cathedral, for example, takes decades, and the edifice is built to last centuries. In Japan, there are no comparable large buildings or public works. Even the famous Toshogu Shrine at Nikko, Tochigi Prefecture, was built in seventeen months. Our ancestors only undertook projects they could finish in their lifetimes.

In the West, time is perceived as an arrow moving rapidly toward a target. Japanese see time unfolding as an endless scroll, without start or end, and the present advances as the scroll uncurls.

Chapter Two

Culture and Management

Culture determines the actions and outlook of individuals and corporations. In a classic definition, the distinguished nineteenth-century anthropologist Edward B. Taylor said: "Culture, or civilization, is that complex whole which includes knowledge, belief, art, law, morals, custom, and any other capabilities and habit, acquired by man as a member of society."[1] All behavior—greetings, table manners, sleeping habits; how people ride an escalator, run a meeting, or reach a consensus—is part of a culture. These forms of behavior are transmitted from generation to generation and evolve over time.

Acculturation begins in early childhood. The English expression "As the boy, so the man" has a counterpart in

[1] Some scholars distinguish between culture and civilization. They include in the former the metaphysical, spiritual, and normative and place in the latter the physical, material and technological. I use "civilization" to refer to a universality that transcends a particular country or cultural community, for example, Greek, Roman, and Chinese civilizations. Not confined to one ethnic group or language, these majestic streams have carried intellectual and aesthetic refinement far beyond their boundaries. A grand civilization can impose common institutions and a way of life on a region of great cultural diversity.

Japanese: "A child's character at three stays with him to age one hundred" (*Mitsugo no tamashi wa hyakusai made tsuzuku*). Individuals (or organizations) that did not share a common early childhood experience face special problems when they interact as adults, whether the situation is a marriage between persons of different nationality, or the Japanese staff of a Tokyo firm's overseas subsidiary negotiating with the local labor force.

Culture

Culture is not in the genes; it is a societal legacy. Through learned behavior human beings have formed languages, created and transmitted knowledge, and shared emotions and ideas. The ability to build and use tools and products has been passed down over the ages. Businesses also inherit a corporate culture which affects their operations, management style, and sales methods. These change somewhat, and new ways are added, as a firm responds to its external environment.

Material culture includes styles in food, clothing, and shelter; spiritual culture subsumes values and normative systems. Individual culture governs a person's attitudes and tastes, while group or organizational culture shapes collective will and work methods. Abstract, internalized values—the conflict between obligation and human passion (*giri* and *ninjō*) to Japanese, or the concept of original sin to Christians—are much harder to change than external, material forms like housing and clothing fashions. Personal attitudes are more resistant to change than public organizational activity.

Revolution can transform political and economic systems, but not ingrained behavior patterns, especially individual attitudes. Authoritarian leaders have tried to coerce cultural change, with evanescent results. When Adolf Hitler rose to power, Germans were required to make the Nazi salute, the raised right arm. They ended letters not with "auf Wiedersehen" but with "Heil Hitler!" In China under

Mao Zedong, people had to carry the little red booklet, *Quotations from Chairman Mao Zedong*, and a common greeting was "Long live Chairman Mao." There was a precedent in China for the presentation of philosophical tenets in one slim volume—the *Analects* of Confucius, which were widely disseminated in earlier centuries. But superficial changes forced on a population never last long. Neither Hitler's fascist hallmarks nor Mao's Little Red Book survived their namesakes.

Government campaigns in Singapore and South Korea to increase productivity are state intervention in the cultural process of value formation. Both countries have adopted a honeybee logo as a symbol of diligence and work: it is used on banners, postage stamps, and theater curtains to sting the populace to greater efforts. Malaysia's "Look East!" campaign likewise is more an attempt at behavior modification than an economic policy. Powerful states generally can penetrate the cultural realm with top-down planning and directives, and some intrusions may prove beneficial. In a mature democratic state, however, government intervention, in the form of curbing freedom of speech or regulating popular customs, is undesirable.

Corporate Culture

When even charismatic leaders and repressive governments have so little impact on basic culture, the task is not likely to be easy for private corporations. Nevertheless, in this age of organizations, corporations and labor unions have an incomparably greater impact on people's spiritual and material lives than in the past. The influence of Big Business in the advanced industrial societies is particularly important.

Companies, especially huge conglomerates, are cultural catalysts in two ways. First, their management methods, planning, and work styles constitute a corporate culture. Second, their products and services, and the advertising that promotes them, affect consumers in the larger society.

Corporate culture, a popular concept in organizational theory of management since the 1970s, is a company's shared values, the norms that determine outlook and behavior. It determines work patterns, with an assist from society.

One litmus test of a corporate culture is whether an employee performs tasks as part of a group or has individual responsibility for a job. In Japan the predominant pattern in all corporate organizations is teamwork. The group is the key unit, not the individual. Japanese are good at collective effort. In assigning a complex project to a five-person unit, management does not divide it into five separate tasks and place one person in charge of each. Usually the five employees are jointly responsible for the entire project. They work together and help each other to accomplish the job.

Although the external cultural environment in Japan favors groupism, corporations are not locked into the prevailing norm. Management can foster individualism. Some years ago I participated in a comparative survey of executives with major corporations in Japan, South Korea, and the Republic of China (Taiwan), hereafter referred to as the JKC Businessmen Survey (see Appendix). We asked this question: Do you prefer to work individually or as part of a team? The response of Japanese employees in various industries is shown in Table 2. Employees of large general trading firms (*sōgō shōsha*) enjoy individual work more than collaboration by a bigger margin than those in other industries. Trading company work seems to attract people with an adventurous spirit.

Table 3 presents the responses of all three nationalities. The data show that Koreans and Chinese are far more individualistic than Japanese, a finding widely endorsed by personal observation and experience.

Table 2. Preference for individual work style over team methods, by industry (%)

Average	36.9%
Light industry	31.5%
Heavy industry	29.5%
General trading firms (*sōgō shōsha*)	47.7%
Finance	36.7%
Wholesalers	43.0%
Large retailers	32.9%

Table 3. Preference for individual work style over team methods, by country (%)

Japan	36.3%
South Korea	51.1%
Republic of China	51.1%

Table 4. Businessmen who favored rule compliance (employee *A*).

Japan	7.4%
South Korea	52.7%
Republic of China	29.7%

In Japan, management emphasizes completion of a task and attainment of objectives over strict adherence to established rules. Pragmatic executives shun bureaucratic red tape and to-the-letter observance of regulations in favor of accomplishing the goal by bending the rules, if necessary, and flexible adjustments.

To probe this aspect, the JKC Businessmen Survey asked the following question: Employee *A* strictly adheres to prescribed work hours. If a task could be accomplished by staying thirty minutes past regular quitting time, he prefers to leave it for the next day and stop work on time. Employee *B* does not feel bound by standard work hours. If a phase of a job can be completed by working thirty minutes extra, *B* will finish it before leaving. Do you approve of *A* or *B*?

The responses (Table 4) show a sharp contrast. Japanese businessmen overwhelmingly endorsed the attitude of employee *B*. Japanese feel very uncomfortable about leaving a task 90 percent finished. A South Korean executive, in contrast does not like to ignore set work hours and continue at a job in the casual style so common in Japanese offices. This is not merely a difference in corporate cultures. The spiritual values of Japan and South Korea determine the choice: the task or the rules.

The younger the respondents were in Japan and the Republic of China, the higher was the support for employee *A*. In South Korea, the opposite was true: approval of employee *B* rose in younger age groups. This divergence intrigued our research team, but space limitations preclude discussion here.

These responses, and others to be discussed below, demonstrate how a societal preference for group collaborative effort is reflected in the work style of a particular organization or enterprise.

Variations in Corporate Culture

Comparisons of management styles in eastern Japan (the Kantō area around Tokyo) with those in western Japan (the Kansai area with Osaka at its center) show that regional milieu also affects organizational modes. Osaka-type management is characterized by the strong independence of merchants, who tend not to ask for government assistance and resist bureaucratic "administrative guidance." They are alert to profitable opportunities, act quickly, and have a short-term outlook. A typical large Tokyo enterprise, in contrast, seeks government aid, follows official "suggestions," and operates on a longer perspective.

Germans from Prussia and Bavaria have different dispositions, yet in national terms we can speak of a Germanic temperament. By the same token executive attitudes in Tokyo and Osaka vary significantly, but they still have much in common that distinguishes them from Westerners, from Chinese, and from Koreans.

Despite the constraints imposed by the special ethos of a society or region, certain enterprises have distinctive corporate cultures that differ from the prevailing patterns. Moreover, there are industry-wide cultures formed by the collective behavior of companies in the same line of business or their trade associations: the Mitsubishi Group, the banking industry, and general trading firms are examples of such distinct corporate cultures.

Each industry, enterprise, and worker is shaped by the norms of society at large as well as of the specific corporate culture. At the same time, however, they are not prisoners bound hand and foot by a cultural web. Even among similar companies in the same sector, a pacesetter grows rapidly, increasing its annual sales year after year, while another firm limps along at a lackluster pace. One company gains a listing on the Tokyo Stock Exchange, and another disappears in bankruptcy proceedings. Performance depends on the special dynamic of each enterprise.

Our survey found significant variation by industry. We asked employees in major Japanese firms the following questions:

1. When a decision is made, is a general and open discussion of the issue important? Or is private consultation (*nemawashi*) preferable? Light-industry employees and wholesalers expressed more support for the open-discussion method; support for *nemawashi* was notably greater in heavy industry.

2. Should company decisions be made by the top echelon/head office, or should decision-making be decentralized to lower levels and branch offices? Wholesalers generally supported the top-level, head-office style; the finance industry showed a marked preference for the lower-echelon, decentralized pattern.

3. Regarding employee performance, is doing one's best sufficient, or is achieving the desired results all that really

counts? To a statistically relevant degree, general trading firm employees endorsed effort regardless of the results; wholesalers said accomplishments are essential.

Responses to questions about ethical issues also show great variation by industry. The survey posed a hypothetical situation, for example: you leave your camera on a park bench, and return to find it gone. Who is more at fault: the person who took it, or you for leaving it behind?

Products and Services

Another dimension of business involvement with culture is the area of products and services. The flow of goods and services into the marketplace, particularly in the advanced industrial societies, chiefly affects the material dimension, the surface, of a culture rather than its core elements. Nevertheless, corporate activities touch every aspect of the lives of contemporary men and women, from the way they brush their teeth and cook food to their deepest emotions.

Corporations create culture every time they introduce a product and differentiate it from existing goods. That process offers the public a choice, a new lifestyle. Consumer markets in the advanced industrial countries are already saturated; basic needs have been fulfilled. The real marketing challenge is to create new needs.

John Wanamaker, the American department store magnate, reportedly originated the practice of giving a present to mothers on Mother's Day. The bonanza for the greeting-card, flower, and candy industries continues today. Japanese retailers have been equally resourceful. November 15 is Shichi-go-san ("Seven-Five-Three Day"), and children of those ages are dressed in their best clothes and taken to visit a shrine. The custom of buying new outfits for children for the event was largely created in this century by Tokyo department stores. They seized upon an old folk practice, an exorcism ceremony on the fifteenth day of the eleventh month for children aged three or seven. By skillful advertising, the department stores manipulated parents into purchasing expensive children's clothing for the occasion. After World War II the practice spread from the Tokyo area to Osaka and ultimately nationwide.

Most gift-giving to relatives or close friends—at the *bon* season in Japan, at *chusok* in South Korea (a Confucian ceremony for ancestors), and the Western celebration of Mother's Day and Father's Day—were created by merchants. Vance Packard catalogued these commercial strategies in the United States in *The Hidden Persuaders.*

Business promotes new products and fashions, incessantly stimulating new consumption patterns. The pocketbook is the target, but value systems are also affected. Sony's Walkman portable cassette tape players enabled people to take music with them on the street, bike, train—almost anywhere. Instant foods made it easier for vast numbers of married women to work outside the household. Throwaway products like paper plates and cups have transformed attitudes. An aversion to waste and a preference for frugality and durability in Japan have given way to acceptance of convenience despite waste. Television has made people more receptive to electronic images than to the printed word, to sensed perception rather than rational presentation.

Yet it is still unclear whether modern marketing techniques are leading the public or are following underlying shifts in tastes. Are marketers "pushing" unwary consumers toward unwanted products, or are consumers "pulling" in a certain direction, with industry and corporations trying to keep up?

The JKC Businessmen Survey asked the following question in Japan: *A* thinks that the fashion industry continuously turns out new styles of clothing, shoes, etc., to stimulate and channel consumer demand. *A* believes that designers, clothing and accessory makers, and the fashion media are the arbiters of public taste. However, *B* believes that fashion moves at its own pace and in its own direction, which commercial interests cannot accelerate or divert. Clothing, footwear, and cosmetics companies frantically turn out products they hope will coincide with public whims. *B* concludes that business does not create mass preferences. With which position do you agree?

A high percentage of respondents from companies in heavy industry and finance which do not make consumer products think that business is the chief instigator of new trends and styles (see Table 5). Yet employees of large retailers who deal directly with the public tend to believe the opposite: that business follows the lead of customers. The correct interpretation is probably midway between these two viewpoints: corporations sometimes create mass tastes and sometimes are at the mercy of a fickle public.

Table 5. Respondents who think "Business creates fashion," by industry

Average	33.4%
By industry	
Light industry	32.0%
Heavy industry	46.3%
General trading firms	36.2%
Finance	47.3%
Wholesalers	20.8%
Large retailers	17.4%
By job group	
General	33.7%
Management	33.0%

Corporations as Cultural Catalysts

Corporations are often the unwitting agents of cultural change. In Britain, people on an escalator who prefer to ascend slowly stand on the right-hand side of the step; the left side is kept open for those persons in a hurry who want to walk up quickly. In Japan, the custom is to not walk or run up an escalator; most people stand on one step until they reach the top.

It is puzzling that Japanese, who are always briskly bustling about, will stand still on an escalator, but the practice is believed to date from before World War II. The first escalators used in Japan were in department stores, whose customers included farmers from the countryside who had never before seen moving stairs. Fearful that these rustic patrons might fall down or become entangled in the machinery, store personnel instructed all passengers to stand still in the middle of the steps and remain that way till they reached the next floor. This became the Japanese way of riding an escalator.

Several years ago the Lotte department store in Seoul, a subsidiary of a Japanese company, installed a new escalator. Female attendants and recorded announcements instructed patrons, à la Japan, to "stand still in the middle of the step." If the store had directed customers to use the escalators in the British way, that would have become the standard pattern throughout South Korea.

Visitors to Japan can soon see what happens when these customs collide. At the New Tokyo International Airport there is a long moving walkway for passengers. Most Japanese stand motionless on it as if it were an escalator, and Westerners walking rapidly ahead often bump into them. Cultural conflict starts within minutes of arrival.

Female employees at the Lotte department store are also trained to bow deeply to customers, the practice in Japan. Seoulites probably find this quite strange. It has not been the custom in Korean shops to greet customers with effusive gestures of appreciation for their patronage; Lotte is introducing a new element into South Korean retailing.[2] Lotte has also introduced background music

[2] In Singapore, too, the staff of a Japanese-owned department store have been trained to bow deeply to patrons. But customers complain: "Instead of

with a faster beat on special sale days. New retail selling methods are pouring into South Korea's business culture.

A major indicator of an economy's commercial development is the shift in the retail trade from a selling price determined by bargaining to a fixed price indicated by a price tag. In Japan the fixed-price system was inaugurated in the sixteenth century by the Mitsui Echigoya kimono store, predecessor of the Mitsukoshi Department Store. Other kimono merchants at the time visited customers' homes to take orders and then delivered the finished goods. Echigoya instituted a system of in-shop cash sales at a fixed price. Their goal was low per-unit profits and quick turnover.

In voluntary commercial transactions, economic efficiency usually wins out. But customs are not necessarily rational and may not easily yield to streamlining innovations. Changing the way a society does business can be a time-consuming process. The self-service method created by U.S. supermarkets spread rapidly to Europe, Japan, the Soviet Union, and the People's Republic of China. However, credit cards have not been as widely accepted. Some business methods have a supra-cultural diffusionability; others are culture-specific. Tradition has ways of defying even universalistic efficiency.

In summary, to understand a corporation or a society, we must look at both the rational processes, such as politics and the economy, and the irrational dimension of culture. Japanese culture was created by our distant ancestors and acquired by later generations as learned behavior. The business world always interacts with the society at large. Corporations are affected by external norms, and, consciously or not, they spread a culture through their products, services, and advertising.

---

the bowing and scraping, we'd rather bargain over prices."

Chapter Three

Culture: The Invisible Barrier

Jumbo jets and microchips have dramatically shrunk the world. A single Boeing 747 winging across the Pacific carries diplomats on a trade liberalization mission, executives pondering joint ventures and off-shore manufacturing deals in half a dozen countries, bankers calculating rates on Eurobonds in the Brussels and Tokyo capital markets, and scholars on their way to conferences on fiber optics or gene-splicing. Many passengers type on silent lap computers. Upon landing, they will send messages by modem to electronic mailboxes or facsimile texts to colleagues around the globe.

Acceptance of national differences in political and economic systems, which are driven by their own internal logic, allows the rapid movement of people and communications between states and business communities. Yet cultural systems, fundamentally irrational and value-ridden, often block real understanding and friendship.

I was part of a Japanese group that visited the People's Republic of China. Chinese officials welcomed us with great cordiality. Our first encounter with Chinese values occurred when the leader of our group was led to a luxury limousine while the rest of us were jammed into a minibus. In Chinese society the leader of an organization has dictatorial authority over his subordinates, and receives preferential treatment. However, to Japanese, who have become accustomed since World War II to egalitarianism, the "leader" is just the person who makes all the arrangements for the group, more a high-grade "gofer" than anything else. Any Japanese who visits the PRC knows ahead of time that it is a socialist country with a planned economy and is bound to be different from capitalist, market-economy Japan. Nevertheless, we were psychologically unprepared for the cultural gap: one member treated like an exalted VIP and the others like lowly plebeians.

We were not the only perplexed foreigners. American visitors to China, with their democratic upbringing, had a similar reaction. One U.S. group rotated their leader daily so each person would get a chance to ride in stretch-limousine comfort. The Chinese reportedly were very angry at such "frivolity." The officials may have interpreted American behavior as a spiteful response to Chinese flunkyism. In any case, the Chinese saw it as a violation of their organizational principles, i.e., their cultural system.

Table manners vary by country and cultural region. Noisily slurping noodles is proper in Osaka and gross in Detroit. Although Chinese and Japanese are neighbors, the two feel somewhat uneasy when dining together. Japanese consider it a breach of etiquette not to carefully arrange one's chopsticks after eating; the Chinese regard a table littered with chopsticks and plates as proof that a guest has dined well. At an official dinner in China all the guests suddenly start to eat. At some point later, when everyone's hunger pangs have been eased, the speeches start. The Chinese believe that no one enjoys listening to a speech with plates of delicious food in front of them that they cannot touch. In Japan, introductions and speeches always precede the eating and drinking at official functions, and even on many social occasions.

Culture is a hidden barrier to economic cooperation between Japanese and Koreans, too. As the JKC Businessmen Survey showed, there can be tension at quitting time between Japanese and Koreans working together in a joint venture over whether to finish up the work at hand or leave at the prescribed time.

Incentives can also be a stumbling block. In the same survey we asked the following question:

> Some people think that if a person makes a contribution to society, some kind of formal recognition—an honorary degree or a medal—is sufficient and a material reward secondary. Other people believe that monetary compensation is preferable, with intangible recognition secondary. With which point of view do you sympathize?

Table 6. Preference for recognition instead of a tangible reward

Japan	46.1%
South Korea	71.7%
Republic of China	56.0%

Responses are presented in Table 6, in the form of percentages of respondents favoring recognition over tangible rewards. Many more South Korean respondents than Japanese chose recognition over tangible rewards. Moreover, the percentage rose with younger Koreans; the younger the Japanese, the stronger the preference for financial reward. These data indicate societal differences that have become more marked since World War II. In Japan, the inauguration of commercial television broadcasting in 1952, with its advertisements for consumer products, spread a desire for wealth and possessions among young people. At the same time, postwar educational reforms eliminated ethics instruction from classrooms because of its association with prewar militarism, thus opening the way for the spread of more materialistic values. In South Korea, on the other hand, while the same technological modernization was taking place, ideological conflicts on the peninsula meant that idealism retained its appeal for younger people as well as older. Thus Koreans are more likely to prefer recognition to monetary rewards. In visits to the offices of South Korean business leaders, I have seen many testimonial statements and trophies proudly displayed. In Japan, senior executives' offices are lined with shelves of books and domestic and foreign magazines. (Whether they have read them all is another matter.)

An organization staffed by an equal number of young Japanese and South Korean employees, thus, is likely to be sharply divided when it comes to deciding on promotions or bonuses. Chinese attitudes fall midway between Japanese and South Korean views on quitting time and compensation (see Tables 4 and 6). A multinational corporation with employees from the three countries might be able to neutralize the differences by making the Chinese view the mean. Although Japanese and South Koreans have similar tastes in popular songs, television dramas, and romantic movies, these data show that in the realm of organizational dynamics and work methods there are sharp cleavages in the underlying cultural and psychological dimensions.

Our survey suggests that management methods vary by culture. Just as there is a Japanese-style management, there is also a South Korean style, and a Country X style. We need to know more about the factors peculiar to each. First we have to decide what constitutes a cultural sphere and then isolate its core element.

What Is a Cultural Sphere?

We often speak of "Japanese culture," "Chinese culture," or "Spanish culture." Is a cultural region marked by the political boundaries of a nation-state's territory? By ethnic group? Do religion or ideology define a cultural sphere? Perhaps language or customs are the key determinants?

It is relatively easy to eliminate national boundaries and ideology as the key factors. Consider the case of divided Germany. Although East and West Germany have very different political and economic systems, in many respects they share a common culture. The buildings and townscapes of the two Germanys have a similar architectural style. Germans on both sides of the border eat nearly the same cuisine. Despite the Cold War and political and economic divergence, one might say "Germanic culture *über Alles*."

Central America and South America are fractionalized into many countries, but their peoples and societies are similar. Conversely, although West Germany and France are both capitalist democracies, they have quite distinct cultures. The Soviet Union and the People's Republic of China belong to the socialist bloc; both have planned economies, and communist parties control political life. Yet culturally, East is East and West is West. Soviet citizens wear suits and neckties and eat with knives and forks; Moscow is materially and spiritually part of Europe. Chinese wear Mao-style clothing and eat with chopsticks; Beijing belongs to Confucian East Asia.

Some large nation-states—China, India, and Indonesia—harbor a great variety of peoples, religions, and cultures. Perhaps the concentration of an ethnic group in an area constitutes a cultural sphere. But there are small countries—Yugoslavia, Switzerland, and Belgium are examples—in which several ethnic groups have created one national culture. On the other hand, the Hindus, Buddhists, and

Parsees in India are the same ethnically, but they are now so divided by religion that they do not intermarry and can be said to have different cultures.

Religion could be the key determinant of culture, except that it often transcends race and culture. Islam stretches from Indonesia and the southern Philippines in the Far East to Morocco in North Africa. Christianity includes among its believers the Caucasians of Europe and North America and the Polynesians of the central and south Pacific. Hinduism, too, with followers in India and eastern Indonesia, has spread across many cultural regions. Mahayana Buddhism has taken root in diverse soil: India, Tibet, China, and Japan. Zones of faith do not conform to cultural spheres.

Language: The Key Determinant of Culture

Culture seems most congruent with language. In Switzerland, Yugoslavia, Canada, China, and the Soviet Union, all of them multiethnic and multilingual nations, each linguistic region has a distinct culture. Thirteen languages are officially recognized in India, and each linguistic group has its own culture.

In a heterogeneous world, Japan is the rare exception: a homogeneous culture. Political boundaries, ethnicity, religion, and language are all congruent. The Japanese language is spoken only in Japan and is the only language spoken there.[1] This linguistic and ethnic unity is due to Japan's geographical position: an archipelago off the Eurasian continent.

[1] The minor exceptions do not compromise this extraordinary correspondence. A small number of emigrants in places outside Japan like Brazil and Hawaii speak Japanese. Some Chinese merchants long resident in Yokohama and Nagasaki speak Chinese, and there are also small ethnic minorities of Ainu, an indigenous people, and Koreans who came to Japan when the peninsula was a Japanese colony (1910–45).

Since the dawn of history the Japanese have never had to flee their islands—have never been refugees. All the peoples of Eurasia and Africa have in historical times, because of war, political upheaval, or natural disaster, left their ancestral lands en masse or lived in exile before finally settling in their present locations. (The United States has been the major magnet for the most recent waves of religious and economic immigrants. This immigrant legacy is the source of the vitality and pioneering spirit that infuses American culture.) The refugee experience continues today as political or religious conditions have compelled exoduses from the Indian subcontinent, Indochina, and parts of Africa.

The Japanese collective subconscious bears no memory of being refugees. We have never been uprooted or suffered the trauma of diaspora. Not surprisingly, the people of this cultural region, formed from a single language, religion, and ethnic group, have unique cultural and behavior patterns.

A shared language gives people a sense of group identity, a feeling of fraternity. The compliment "He speaks my language" means that the person "shares my attitudes and values." Because a common language encourages a sense of national identity, every modern state sooner or later advocates the use of a single official tongue. That policy offends ethnic minorities and provokes separatist movements, since to accept a language is to assimilate. The first generation of Japanese emigrants to the United States, for example, communicated with their associates and families in Japanese. As long as they used it, their attitudes and behavior still bore traces of their roots. But the second, third, and fourth generations, who have lost that fluency, are now thoroughly Americanized.

Acquired through imitation, practice, and education, language enables members of a group to communicate and perceive their collective unity. It is a means of thought, a tool of intellect. When people learn a language, they also learn new ground rules for reason and cognition. True command of two or more languages should make an individual bicultural or multicultural.

Language, including non-verbal body language, is the foundation of culture. According to specialists in linguistics, the language a person learns and uses until about age 20 becomes his mother tongue, the bedrock of his primary culture. A language spoken at an earlier age, when the ego is not yet developed, is completely forgotten by adulthood unless it is used through late adolescence. After a person is 20, any new language will always be "foreign," and knowledge acquired with it will remain part of a different culture.

The importance of the interface of language and culture can scarcely be overstated. A society's reaction to foreign concepts is often mirrored in language. The general response of Japanese, Koreans, and Chinese to the West in the nineteenth century can be seen in a mundane example: what they called a certain beverage—beer.

Japanese: *bí-i-rŭ*
Korean: *maek-ju*
Chinese: *pí-jiŭ*

Japanese are open and receptive to foreign things, so there was no linguistic resistance. We followed the original pronunciation and wrote "beer" in *kana*. Although eclectic, in the fullness of time Japanese will blend the extrinsic item into their own culture. As ビール, it is perceived as a Japanese term, not a foreign loan word.

Koreans, with their phonetic han'gul writing system, could have written beer as 비이유 (*bi-i yu*), but this is rarely done. Instead, a Korean equivalent was chosen—*maekju*.[2]

[2] *Maekju* comes from the Chinese words *mai* (barley) and *jiu* (liquor). Strictly speaking, *maekju* is not a pure Korean word but a borrowing from Chinese.

Compared to Japanese, the Koreans have been wary of foreign culture, an attitude they share with the French. Both peoples are proud and stubborn about their language.

The Chinese coined their own equivalent for beer. The first character, pronounced *pí*, is new *kanji* made by joining the characters for "mouth" (口) and "humble" (卑). Then the character for liquor, 酒, read *jiŭ*, was added to signify "humble mouth liquor." The compound implies that it is a beverage drunk by backward people like Westerners, crude barbarians outside the scope of Chinese civilization. From ancient times the Han people regarded those around them as primitives and labelled them with characters that denoted contempt.

The way the three countries translated "beer" was typical of their response to Western culture in the nineteenth century. (Let's defer judgment for the moment on which reaction shows élan.) Scornful of the West, after the Opium War (1839–42) China lost part of its territory to the European powers and Japan, and failed to modernize. Korea continued to regard China as the suzerain culture and ridiculed Japan's westernization, but suffered the bitter fate of becoming a Japanese colony. Japan gulped down Western ideas and technology with the same alacrity it adopted the word "beer." Although a late starter, Japan quickly made the transition from feudalism to capitalism, and catching up with the West became a national goal. The unusual quality of Japanese culture was manifested in this process: eager acceptance of things foreign combined with defense of the traditional. (I shall discuss how this characteristic affects management techniques in Chapter 4.)

However, Koreans think of it as indigenous. That misperception itself shows the extent to which Chinese language and culture were assimilated during the centuries when Korea was a cultural vassal of the Middle Kingdom.

Formation of Japan's Unique Culture

When was Japan's unique culture formed? It dates from the time when the people on the archipelago began to use a single language. According to Japan's pioneer cultural anthropologist Ishida Ei'ichirō (1903–68), archaeological research places this development from at least the Yayoi period (200 B.C. to A.D. 250); whether Jōmon man (? to 200 B.C.) spoke Japanese is unknown. The *Wei Zhi* (*Wei-chih*), a third-century Chinese historical work, has a section on the people of Wa, the early designation for Japan. Ishida says that several words in this record are "attempts to record the pronunciation of the Japanese language of that time."[3] One is *hinamori*, an old idiomatic word for a border guard. Word order and other linguistic traces prove that Yayoi man spoke the original form of modern Japanese.

A culture's leitmotif is shaped in the formative years of a people, much as the core personality of an individual is set in childhood. If Professor Ishida's hypothesis is correct, the traits of Japanese and the character of our culture today had already been formed in the Yayoi period. We do not know if the society was patriarchal or matriarchal, nor whether the Yayoi people were farmers, seafarers who came to the islands from the south, or nomads who crossed over from North Asia. But on these islands, our ancestors grew rice in paddy fields and lived in villages. They had started to form the idiosyncracies of Japanese-style organizations and management. At least in the Western part of the archipelago, Yayoi people definitely spoke Japanese.

According to Ishida, "For a time, southern Korea and western Japan formed a closely related cultural sphere that

[3] This and other quotations in this chapter are from *Japanese Culture: A Study of Origins and Characteristics* by Ei'ichirō Ishida, trans. by Teruko Kachi (University of Tokyo Press, 1974).

was almost a single unit." Later developments made the Tsushima Straits between Kyushu and Korea a dividing line. On the Japan side, the Yayoi people began to mix with the descendants of the Jōmon people, who were located mainly in eastern Honshu. Across the straits, southern Korea became unified with the northern part of the peninsula.[4]

Throughout history nomadic and mounted tribes, the ancestors of Westerners, have eschewed manual labor. They exploited draft animals and conquered agricultural peoples. The nomads and riders saw themselves as rulers fitted for mental tasks like military strategy, scholarship, and politics. Their descendants gave the world imperialism, colonialism, the Industrial Revolution, and modern technological civilization. Westerners love liberty and select their leaders democratically; this elite runs the society. To have hereditary leaders or managers like those favored by agricultural peoples might have endangered a cattle-raising or hunting society. Regardless of whether the peoples who settled on

[4] The origin of the Japanese is an issue perhaps best left to historians. The most persuasive of the many theories is that the Jōmon people came from the south and settled in the islands in the fifth to third century B.C. Later another people, either from the northern part of the Asian mainland or the descendants of horseriders, arrived from Korea and drove the original settlers to the east and north. Evidence of such a population shift remains today. For example, from a point north of Morioka, Iwate Prefecture, all mice have the same genes as mice in Taiwan, the Philippines, and South China; all mice south of Morioka have a genetic structure identical to those in North China, Manchuria, and Korea. If people and mice moved eastward at the same time, then this fact endorses the migration hypothesis. In anthropological terms, the earlier residents are dolichocephalic—relatively long-headed—and belong to the schizoid type; the latecomers are brachycephalic—short- or broad-headed—and classified as manic-depressive. (One fascinating theory holds that most of the dynamic, outstanding figures in Japanese history since the population shift were of the latter type). Japanese music today is based on a two-part time, whereas Korean music has a three-part time. These times are believed to have been adopted when the basic culture was formed. The two-beat pronunciation of words in eastern Japan and three-beat pronunciation in western Japan is a vestige of this early stage.

the Japanese archipelago were originally farmers or livestock-raising hunters, over the course of 2,000 years on these islands, so fertile and secure from powerful enemies, they gradually became sedentary agricultural folk.

The formative stage of Japanese culture lasted until about A.D. 200–300. (In terms of American history this corresponds to the century from 1776 to 1876 when the country was geographically unified and its prototypical culture was shaped.) The main grammar rules of the Japanese language were probably completed at this time. Villages and hamlets surrounded by rice-growing paddy fields became the archetype of Japanese culture.

Culture Shock

Each cultural sphere in the world today was established under distinctive conditions; once mature, its character, like a human personality, is unchangeable or highly resistant to transformation. Contemporary men and women are the descendants of rice farmers and hunters, villagers and nomads, mountain tribes and oceangoing sailors. When peoples of such radically different origins interact, misunderstanding and trouble invariably occur. At the personal level we call this culture shock.

Short of avoiding all interaction across cultural boundaries, there are three ways to deal with cultural dissonance. In the first way, one side accepts the other as the dominant culture, studies its history and customs, and adjusts its own behavior accordingly. In the second way, one party compels the other to accept its culture by *force majeure*. History shows many cases where a large, populous country imposes its will on a small, weak country. The process is often brutal and unjust. In either case, it is relatively easy to learn the superficial material aspects of the dominant culture; the emotional dimension of social norms and spiritual values is more complex and elusive. Work methods and criteria for rewards and punishment, nurtured by societies over a long period and in particular historical circumstances, often prove baffling.

Both of these two patterns are unilateral and arbitrary: only one side does the learning and adjusting. No one can objectively decide that value *A* is correct and logical whereas value *B* is wrong and irrational. Nor should a majority culture be forced on a minority.

The third way to reduce intercultural conflict is a mutual effort at understanding and an attitude of cultural relativism. This approach prevents some trouble and usually keeps tempers below the boiling point. Faced with a totally different culture, everyone hesitates at first. Enthusiastic acceptance of strange ways is blocked by natural caution toward the unknown or fear of failure. But a rigorous commitment to objectivity and fairness can overcome inhibitions. And it is an intellectually exciting challenge that many people, some in exalted positions, are meeting throughout the world. Pope John Paul II, for example, engages in dialogue on a basis of equality not only with Protestants but also with Islamic and Buddhist leaders.

Tolerance and reciprocity are relatively easy for world leaders and intellectuals but not for the general population. There is always friction when people of different backgrounds live in close proximity. Millions of "guest workers" (*Gastarbeiter*) from Turkey and Eastern Europe have settled in West Germany since the period of rapid economic growth in the 1960s. When the economy was growing spectacularly, they were welcomed and praised for their contribution to the "German miracle." Later, as the boom faded and unemployment rose, they were regarded as a nuisance, a horde of unassimilated outsiders. In a bitter emotional backlash, some Germans now charge that the "guests" make no effort to be assimilated. The evidence cited is trivial. Turkish women walking along the street with scarves on their heads are an "eyesore," Germans say. Turkish couples do not dine out together because social life is sexually segregated, some Germans complain. Faced with this hostility, Turks live in ethnic ghettos where store signs are in Turkish and the atmosphere is more Oriental than European. It is a vicious circle: crowding together into such neighborhoods causes even more social problems, which intensify German dislike.

In the United States, almost all ethnic groups are newcomers; some just arrived sooner than others. U.S. society is an ethnic crucible, as the Japanese archipelago was in the third century A.D. when the Jōmon and Yayoi peoples were assimilating. Most immigrants in America have not faced the wall of prejudice and rejection that surrounds Turkish communities in West Germany. However, if the large-scale illegal influx of non-English-speaking people from Mexico, Central America, and the Caribbean continues, Hispanics may find themselves as unwelcome as the Turks are in Germany.

Japanese emigrants to the United States early in this century had a relatively weak sense of cultural identity and sought assimilation. This desire to fit in triggered reactions of emotional Caucasian prejudice against Orientals. But the Japanese did not all crowd together in ethnic neighborhoods or associate only with one another. They earned a reputation as industrious and law-abiding, and were gradually accepted as full-fledged Americans.[5] Their experience shows that flexibility is the catalyst of cultural fusion.

[5] Two cultural characteristics of Japanese immigrants facilitated their transition: unassertiveness and openness. In the past Chinese and Japanese both established "Chinatowns" and "Little Tokyos" in Indochina, the Philippines, Malaysia, and Indonesia. Although the Chinese residential areas still flourish, all the Japanese sections are gone. One major reason reportedly is that the Japanese intermarried with indigenous peoples and the ethnic community broke up. Also, Japanese do not have a strong sense of religion, which often

Control of key economic functions or occupations by an unassimilated ethnic group intensifies antipathy. Overseas Chinese dominate the distribution of commodities and merchandise throughout Southeast Asia, and Indians have a similar grip on the east coast of Africa. In Malaysia, the proportion of Malays, Chinese, and Indians in the population is five, four, and one, respectively. The three groups have different lifestyles, occupations, and religious affiliations; ethnic antagonisms have led to outbursts of communal violence in the past. Chinese economic ascendancy particularly rankles indigenous Malays, and the Malay-dominated government puts constant pressure on the dynamic Chinese minority. In recent years the three peoples have realized they must live together and have begun, somewhat

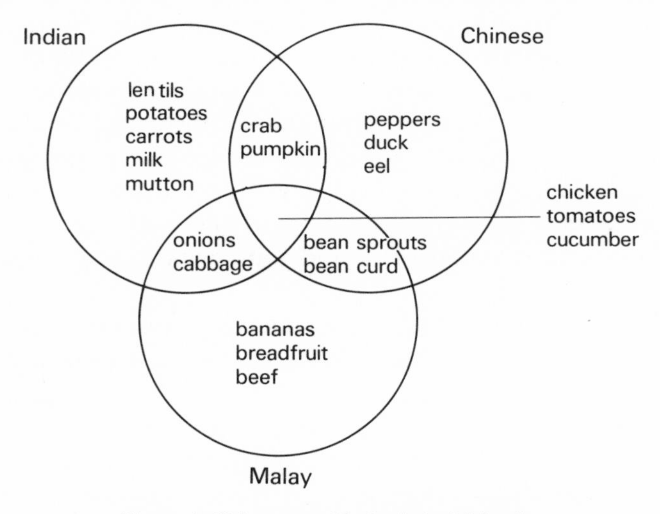

Figure 4. Culture-specific foods in Malaysia.

engenders solidarity among expatriates. Chinese share this relative disinterest in faith, but their family is a powerful, coherent unit. Many small ethnic groups have preserved their identity in Central Asia by not intermarrying with other peoples. German settlers in Latin America are said to maintain their customs and language for generations; Japanese immigrants quickly melt into the local society.

fatalistically, to try to make coexistence work. Now, when college students in Malaysia hold a party or social function, for example, different foods are often laid out on separate tables for each ethnic group. About the only foods eaten by all are chicken and tomatoes (Figure 4). (Similarly, certain cities and factories in China have separate dining areas for Muslims, in which pork, a Chinese favorite, is replaced by chicken.)

Interaction between groups with different cultural backgrounds is fraught with tension. In a homogeneous society like Japan, which for many centuries had only limited contact with foreigners and whose members are not accustomed to commercial or diplomatic dealings with outsiders, it is arduous at best and traumatic at worst.

Business organizations constitute a man-made, structured system unlike an autogeneous society. Corporations can function abroad with relative ease because so much is replicated: companies (both allies and competitors), products, a distribution system, annoying government regulations, and afternoons on the golf course where deals are made. Nevertheless, culture intrudes, and many of the failures of multinational enterprises and joint ventures are due to cultural dissonance.

For both an individual and a society, the price of avoiding contact with another party from fear of misunderstanding is very high: a missed chance for genuine friendship. Disagreement is frequently the first step to enlightenment, and many a good relationship begins with a faux pas. Japanese corporations often disrupt overseas markets by underpricing the competition ("dumping"); foreign companies in Japan violate custom and outrage employees by suddenly stopping operations and dismissing everyone. But if in the long run these commercial activities make us more sensitive to one another, they will benefit Japan and its trading partners.

The Third Opening

As Japan looks to the twenty-first century, we need a third opening to the world that finally ends our isolation and leads to assimilation in the global community. The first opening was in 1853 when Commodore Matthew C. Perry's four-vessel squadron, called the "Black Ships" by alarmed Japanese, sailed into Uraga in Edo (Tokyo) Bay. Subsequent negotiations led to the United States–Japan Treaty of Friendship and Commerce in 1858. The Treaty of Aigun between Russia and China, signed the same year, extended Russian territory to the Pacific. In India the Sepoy mutiny was raging against British rule. Against this tense backdrop of Western intrusion and Asian resistance, Japan was opened to the world. The Powers banged on the door, and Japan very reluctantly said, "Come in."

This political opening proved enormously beneficial to Japan: it turned a decentralized feudal polity into a modern nation-state. Two hundred fifty years of seclusion during the Tokugawa shogunate and several thousand years of isolation imposed by geography ended as Japan cautiously emerged from its cocoon into the outside world.

The second opening, an economic one, dates from 1960; it was characterized by liberalization of commodity trade, capital, and finance. Perceived as a second attack by the West, it was resisted by protectionist roadblocks and stalling. Just as we had a century earlier, we acted only because of pressure from the other industrialized nations. Yet again the results were enormously favorable to Japan. We should have voluntarily liberalized our economy, not made niggling, piecemeal concessions to placate trading partners. But long benign isolation, coupled with abundant agricultural and marine resources, has made Japanese exclusivist by habit.

Japan now faces a third opening, this time a cultural

widening of society and individual attitudes. We have achieved an international reputation for first-rate industrial products ranging from videocassette recorders and automobiles to machine tools and turbines. But only a fraction of Japan's spiritual culture has been exported to the world. Exotic anachronisms like samurai and geisha still present a distorted image of this society.

Just as Japanese were unwilling to expose their polity and economy to foreign influences, we have been disinclined to open this village (*mura*) society to outsiders. To be candid, we hated the prospect. There have been a few notable exceptions who worked to spread Japan's culture abroad: art critic Okakura Tenshin (1862–1913), Zen philosopher Suzuki Daisetsu Teitaro (1870–1966), and cultured pearl developer Mikimoto Kōkichi (1858–1954). Most of the population, however, were indifferent or rejected the idea of making Japanese culture accessible to outsiders. Some masked ethnocentrism in arrogance, boasting that "Japan's superior culture is unequalled anywhere in world." Others said, "Foreigners cannot be expected to appreciate our culture, no matter how much we try to explain it" (superiority complex), or "An unusual culture like Japan's will be misunderstood and laughed at" (inferiority complex).

In recent years, however, Zen, flower arrangement, the tea ceremony, Kabuki, Noh, traditional music, and literature have been well received overseas. Many artifacts from our daily lives have also gained an appreciative foreign audience. American and French cooking, for example, have adopted many ingredients and ways of presenting food from Japanese cuisine. Japanese paper has earned plaudits for durability. (After a century the pages of the average book printed in the West fall apart; traditional Japanese paper has been known to last more than 1,000 years.) Although our distinctive architectural style is unsuited to other climates, many features have been highly praised: the adaptability to temperature changes—sliding doors that open to the outside—and the use of natural materials—wood, paper, and straw.

Japan's industrial and business methods have also been acclaimed. Many U.S. business schools teach about small work units in factories and the total quality control (TQC) movement. Foreign executives, seeing in Miyamoto Musashi's book on samurai swordsmanship, *The Book of Five Rings*, an allegory for competition in business, bought the English translation in best-selling numbers. Japan has much to teach the world about social organizations, labor relations, and urban crime control.[6]

A major aspect of Japan's third opening must be a responsiveness to other peoples. Being a homogeneous population, Japanese are extremely wary, to the point of outright refusal, of accepting people of other nationalities into their society. The unwillingness to admit the "boat people" from Indochina after the Vietnam War was a striking example. The nations of Europe and North America, with a history of emigration and acceptance of refugees, empathized with the displaced Vietnamese and agreed to resettle large numbers of them. Japan refused to allow refugees to stay permanently. When other countries criticized Tokyo, the government reluctantly accepted a small number of Indochinese. The West has recognized, in principle, the movement of people from one country to another. Western societies have been opened to outsiders. This does

[6] Police boxes (*kōban*) are branch stations located in urban neighborhoods staffed twenty-four hours a day by one or two policemen. They investigate crimes, help pedestrians find destinations (addresses are not numbered consecutively; a detailed map or help from a local policeman is essential), and maintain close contact with the community. Singapore Premier Lee Kuan Yew learned of the *kōban* system during a visit to Japan. He quickly established it in Singapore and street crime dropped dramatically. The system was also tried in São Paulo, Brazil, but reportedly it did not deter purse snatchers.

not mean there are no restrictions, of course. However, Japanese society is, in principle, closed to outsiders. Exclusion is advocated and stubbornly defended by the government itself. Countless organizations like labor unions, university faculties, and local communities staunchly oppose allowing foreigners into the society. The Ministry of Education, for example, did not permit national universities to hire foreigners for permanent faculty positions until 1983 when the Diet revised the law.

Japanese like to form intimate, exclusive groups composed of people all from the same native place or graduates of the same school. People from different prefectures or colleges are excluded from such groups. The dislike of foreigners with blond or kinky hair and blue eyes is much more intense. Recently, internationalism has become a fad in Japan. Many prefectures and localities have announced that they welcome foreign students and have built "apartments exclusively for foreign-student use." Although traditional Japanese hospitality requires that guests from a distant land be provided with special accommodations, the mentality behind "exclusive" housing is a desire to isolate foreigners. The model is Dejima, a 130-acre artificial island in Nagasaki harbor where first Portuguese and later Dutch traders were confined. From 1641 to 1856, Dejima was the only place the Dutch were allowed to reside. Movement to and from the island was strictly controlled; Westerners were effectively cut off from contact with Japanese. There is still a subconscious desire to keep foreigners at arm's length. Housing foreign and Japanese students in the same dormitory would be the cosmopolitan and friendly thing to do. But our educators and administrators find this notion incomprehensible.

Once again, vigorous external pressure may compel the society gradually to allow significant numbers of outsiders to study, work, and live in Japan. As in the two previous crises, this transformation should bear dividends for Japanese. Instead of waiting for the door to be knocked down, we have to open it ourselves and say "Welcome! Come on in."

The first opening, entailing enormous legal and political innovations, was the government's responsibility. The second impacted on the economy and industry; the adjustments were mainly accomplished by financial and business leaders. Although the third opening—the liberalization of our culture, people, and organizations—depends in part on leadership by government and business, ultimately it is the responsibility of each individual citizen.

At many crucial points in Japan's history, sound decisions and effective government actions saved the nation: the Mongol Invasions (1274 and 1281); the policy of national seclusion in the early 17th century; and the Meiji Restoration (1868). Japan was relatively isolated and insignificant when these events occurred. Mistakes would only have been calamitous for this society. Today Japan is an economic superpower, accounting for 10 percent of the world's gross national product, and our actions have widespread repercussions.

Since the 1960s there has been a quantum increase in Japan's international involvement. Most intercultural activities before that time were at the government and business community level. Henceforth the interface will be increasingly between families and individuals, as Japanese travel more overseas for pleasure, work, and education. They need accurate, objective information about other cultures. Understanding what we have in common will help us respect the unfamiliar and make it possible to synthesize the compatible elements into a new form of civilization.

Chapter Four

Groupism: The Whole and Its Parts

Groupism sets the tone of Japanese-style management and organizational behavior. An imprecise and easily misunderstood concept, groupism should not be confused with totalitarianism. Webster's Third New International Dictionary defines it as "the tendency to think and act as members of a group . . . to conform to the cultural pattern of a group at the expense of individualism. . . ." Individualism and groupism are prototypical American and Japanese patterns, respectively. In the former, the struggle for organizational and economic goals occurs through a confrontation of autonomous individuals who compete in a fierce clash of personalities. In the latter, relatively equal persons form groups to combine their energies and skills and advance the organization's interests. This dichotomy can also be called autonomy versus mutual cooperation.

The leitmotif of Japanese culture that underlies organizational behavior can be traced to the Yayoi period of two thousand years ago. Groupism developed in the idiosyncrasies of an isolated, stable society based on paddy-field rice cultivation.

Cultural concepts

The terms *ie* and *mura* are key concepts in describing Japanese organizations, and their interrelationship is central to groupism. The *ie* is like the state or the official political party in a totalitarian system. The *ie* demands the sacrifice of self-interest to the group's welfare. In certain cases, such as military service, the obligation is compulsory and enforced by sanctions. The concept of *mura*, or village community, is another often used in talking about a family, neighborhood, or business firm. It suggests a community that ostracizes nonconformers but does not compel sacrifice.

In contemporary Japan, an *ie* is a house or dwelling, and by extension a family or home. The word is etymologically related to *iho*, an old word for an umbrella-like covering over a dwelling. According to the oldest official history, *Nihon Shoki* (Chronicle of Japan), after the legendary first emperor, Jimmu, conquered regions along the Inland Sea and decided on Kashihara, Nara Prefecture, as his capital, he used the word *ie* in an imperial edict to announce that all these territories were under his "roof," i.e., under his control.

The term *ie* is associated with the rise of the samurai class and the struggle of military families to survive in medieval Japan. The first samurai were the local farmers, many in eastern Japan, who formed armed groups and contested control of manors by the court nobility in the late twelfth century. They organized around a leader, formed an *ie* which became their stronghold, and defended their land. The *ie* fought to expand their landholdings, and some gradually became quite large. These were led by feudal lords, or *daimyo*. All the samurai affiliated with an *ie* rallied to its defense. If necessary, the loyal warrior gave his life to defend his patron. Today the phrase refers to a person's primary organization. If a company faces a serious crisis, for example, no matter what the personal cost or inconvenience, all employees (samurai) must defend the *ie* group.

The *ie* concept is a special Japanese way of looking at situations when someone—the head of a household, a company president, a political leader—is trying to inspire people to accomplish goals. It is frequently used to explain the relationship between the parts and the whole.

Mura means village or community and comes from a Korean word *maul* (village). It is said to be related to the Japanese verb *mureru*, to crowd together, throng. The *mura* concept indicates a peculiarly Japanese form of social unity. It evokes an image of an agricultural community, closed to outsiders, whose central concern is the mutual benefit of its members. Within a *mura*, personal relationships are intimate; members are relaxed and unguarded with each other. In Hall's terminology, it is a "high-context" environment, "one in which most of the meaning is in the context while very little is in the transmitted message." Through daily contact, communal work, and kinship ties, members have an enormous amount of "stored information" about one another. Verbal communication is often minimal or unnecessary; gestures or tone of voice amply convey meaning.

What happens between next-door neighbors is soon known to everyone. This intimacy has contradictory consequences. On the one hand, all actions are fraught with tension lest one give offense or embarrass one's family, since everybody will hear about it. On the other hand, it is a relaxed society without guile or pretense because no one is afraid that a village scandal or secret will be revealed to outsiders. Even if *mura* members know that one of their number has done something wrong—for example, violated a national law—they will collusively feign ignorance.

Although outsiders are not readily accepted, if a person is once allowed into the community, he or she is accorded full-fledged membership. Discrimination ceases, and the newcomer is treated as an intimate.

Traditionally, a *mura* member who got into relatively minor trouble outside the community was protected by the group. But if the transgression was so serious that it endangered order in the village and could not be justified to the outside world, the offender was ostracized (*murahachibu*) and had to leave. In other cases, a person who violated the village's rules was judged by a meeting of the whole community, and in grave cases he or she was forbidden contact with other villagers. Ostracism was a common practice until the nineteenth century. Community solidarity was very strong, and this was a devastating psychological and physical sanction. Even today, if one member of a group complains about or protests a collective decision, other members shun him, a practice called *murahajiki*, or exclusion from the village. This is a terrible disgrace.

Foreign companies often complain that non-tariff barriers block their entry into the Japanese market. Their problem is that a traditional *mura* society—the Japanese business community—will not admit them as members. *Mura* society is wary of outsiders: they are unknown quantities and potentially disruptive. The would-be member must speak the community's language, and there must be a guarantee that the newcomer will observe its customs and rules. A foreign company seeking access to Japan's distribution channels should refrain from criticizing procedures and requirements that seem illogical and follow all the *mura*'s—traditional Japan's—rules. To achieve market entry requires the patience of Job, but many foreign enterprises expect instant membership in a club that has been closed for centuries.

In an actual village, members lack the clear awareness of their relationship to the whole that an *ie* member has. Their sense of self-identity is weaker. A village also has no objective perception of other *mura* or organizations. The prototypical *mura* is just a group of like-minded people whose goal is mutual prosperity—a good rice harvest, for example. Members are born, marry, and die in the same village. There is no collective sense of where the *mura* stands in the larger cosmos.

It can be argued that Japan has always been one large *mura*-like community. From before the dawn of history Japan was a remote Shangri-la or the fabulous "island in the eastern ocean," Zipangu, that Marco Polo described. Japanese blissfully ignored the rise and fall of tribes and empires on the Eurasian continent that set millions of people in search of safe refuge. Lacking any clear image of the outside world or how to deal with it, we passed more than two placid millennia on this archipelago.

As long as no outside enemy threatens the *mura*, the group does not need a powerful leader. A village headman who maintains *wa* (peaceful harmony) is sufficient. He functions as a manager and mediator, the guardian of community customs. I call him a village headman rather than a leader because ordinarily he does not supervise or direct *mura* residents.

If a village clashes with an external foe and its very existence is endangered, someone must unify the organization to meet the crisis. Strong leadership is needed. Frequently the village headman, in order to function as group leader, applies the *ie* concept to pull the *mura* together. He urges the people: "We've got to band together and fight." It is the same appeal that brought samurai running to the defense of their fief. The *ie* ideal, which relates the individual to the organization, is congenial to the Japanese mentality. When the *mura* or its major interests are at risk, the community instantly functions like an *ie*, makes the *mura* head the leader, and achieves a cohesive unity.

If the leader has the personal magnetism to create a feeling of solidarity—the collective harmony (*wa*) of the village—it is relatively easy for him to use the *ie* appeal to unify opinion and lead it into the fray.

In the absence of external danger, the *mura* head's basic role is to adjust the conflicts that arise among members. The post requires moral suasion and credibility. He should have no enemies in the village and should be endowed with a judicious sense of fairness. The headman in a *mura* society is an able mediator for the masses and rules by character, judgment, and charisma. Ideally, he pulls together an amorphous consensus; he does not personally shape it or influence the group. Strictly speaking, the headman cannot be called a leader.

The Whole and Its Parts

The epistemology of the relationship between the whole and its parts helps to explain the *ie* concept of the link between the organization and the individual. There is a basic difference between how Japanese and Westerners perceive an entity and its elements, a group and its members. The Western way of thinking is precisely stated in the mathematical axiom "The whole is equal to the sum of all its parts." This principle is the basis for consensus or collective action by Westerners.

By contrast, the dominant perception in Japan is that "the whole is more than the sum of its parts." We are taught this from childhood; it is constantly reinforced in the family, at school, and at work, and it permeates the fabric of our culture. In the West, Gestalt psychology emphasizes "wholes," the organization of sensory experiences into "temporal and spatial totalities." Kurt Lewin (1890–1947), a prominent Gestaltist, saw wholes much the way Japanese do, but this is not the mainstream of Western thought. Western science and philosophy teach that to understand the truth of a thing, the totality must be broken down into its parts. Broadly speaking, this analytical method has been used in scientific thinking ranging from Euclidian geometry to the modern natural sciences like physics and biology and the social sciences such as economics. Applying the same principle, Frederick Taylor discovered scientific management by breaking steelworkers' jobs into parts—the famous time-and-motion studies. Taylor's technique of dividing everything into its components is closely linked to the idea that "the *wa* of the parts is the whole."

Americans use the same approach to devise management strategy. They dissect all elements of a problem, assess each factor objectively, and then calculate the advantages and disadvantages of a course of action. Company policy is decided on the basis of cost-benefit analysis. A traditional Japanese company did not—and still does not—use this process, although some Japanese management specialists do recommend U.S.-style decision making, finding it inexplicable that our companies can use less rigorous methods and still be reasonably successful.

The Japanese outlook may be common to all Orientals, and perhaps explains why Western-style science did not develop in Asia. Japanese believe that the essence of a thing is found not in the details but in the whole; we are relatively unconcerned about the elements. We prefer direct, sudden insight. Zen Buddhism relies on disciplined intuitive breakthroughs. Even writing and words are merely symbolic expressions.

In science, philosophy, and everyday life, Japanese have an aversion to breaking things down into minute components for evaluation. With personnel assessments, for example, we dislike quantitative, short-term ratings. Personnel officers prefer to do a qualitative long-term, overall appraisal. Although personal evaluations are kept confidential and appear to contain no negative comments, they are a factual, comprehensive description of the individual. This holistic approach stems from the nature of Japanese society as a vast *mura* in which no privacy is allowed. The members of a high-context community are naked to each other. They talk plainly and openly without the protective veil of evasion or dissembling.

This emphasis on the total relationship permeates Japanese society. Consider how patrons are charged in a sushi restaurant or the red-lantern (*akachōchin*) kind of drinking/eating place men stop at after work. Neither the customer nor the proprietor says anything about the price of individual items on the bill. Both sides avoid an analytical item-by-item breakdown. A customer may feel that the total bill is too high, but he pays the requested amount, praises the food, and leaves without complaint. Instead, the next time the customer says, "You know, last week it seemed a little expensive. But I've gone out of my way to patronize your shop again, so give me a bit of a break today." The proprietor *invariably* replies: "Well, I'm sorry about last time. The weather at sea was bad then and the catch was small. At the fish market that morning everything was expensive, so . . . Today there was plenty of fish and I got a good deal." Neither customer nor shop owner thinks of the bill as a one-time transaction; they prefer an equitable arrangement that sustains the relationship over time. The total situation—past, present, and future—is the basis for mutual agreement. Both parties dislike a transactional nexus that starts and ends with each meal and is calculated from the price of each piece of fish totalled up into a bill. They live by the logic of "the long run."

Prospective employees are not viewed as multifunctional cyborgs from whom a company purchases a single skill such as riveting or selling ability. The corporation and the new employee both understand that the firm hires the whole individual. Management does not lay off workers during a business slump because it has accepted them into the fold. That relationship cannot be severed just because the workers' labor is not needed at one particular time. This is the *ie* consciousness in practice.

In theory and practice, Japanese tend to think of the whole—the company or nation—rather than its components. The totality becomes a value greater than its parts. The individual's welfare is relatively unimportant; the *ie* is supreme, the great cause for whose survival and prosperity group members are prepared to sacrifice.

Groupism versus Totalitarianism and Individualism

Although groupism seems to be a characteristic of Germans, their version differs from the Japanese *ie* variety in recognizing the existence of independent atom-like individuals. The German pattern is totalitarian because in a mass society of atomized individuals there must be a Führer, or leader, who pulls everyone together. It might be said that Germans believe the whole is meaningful only because of the parts, while Japanese think the parts are meaningless without the whole. Adolf Hitler called himself Führer, and Germans even call a tour group guide a "*Reise Führer.*" In Japan, the title is "tour attendant" or "tour escort," and the person is a kind of mother hen to a *mura* group. Dictators like Hitler gain the support of the masses, who are a collection of atoms, and promise sweeping changes and improvements. There have been many violent tyrants in Asia, including Japan, but there was never a Western-style dictator until Mao Zedong. The Great Helmsman owed his rise to power to the Chinese Communist Party and its Western ideology of Marxism.

In Western thinking, everything begins with the individual; the whole consists of discrete human beings. This is true of American management theory, whether it deals with formal organizational structure or emphasizes informal human relations. Basic human rights, which stress the value of the individual, originated in the West; it was not a universal concept. The notion of human rights posits a logical distinction and fundamental conflict between the interests of an organization and its individual members. The problem is seen as rights in conflict, and the answer is to somehow adjust the competing claims of the individual and the community, be it the nation or a voluntary association like a corporation. In Japan, although the immediate interests of the individual and the group (family, village, company) may seem to diverge, it has always been thought that they converge in the larger imperative of survival for the company or nation. Goals merge in long-term interests, a common destiny. The mainstream of Oriental philosophy, including Japan's belief systems in Japan, holds that there is ultimately no contradiction between the whole and its parts, between the individual and the family, kinship group, community, and nation. Where Western philosophy sees unavoidable conflict, Eastern thought finds a final harmony.

I have been contrasting "East" and "West," an ancient dichotomy. Some readers may object that a discussion based on a simple division of the vast Eurasian continent into two geographical regions is unscholarly. To forestall such objections, I want to define the areas and explain why they are so meaningful.

I find it useful, following a boundary suggested by Professor Ishida Ei'ichirō, to regard the area east of Burma, Tibet, and China as the "East" and include India and the Middle East in the "West." Although the inclusion of the Middle East in the West may seem dubious, I do it because, with a few exceptions like Hungary and Finland, the peoples who live west of India speak Indo-European languages. These predominantly Caucasoid peoples have formed societies with castes or caste-like distinctions. By contrast, the peoples to the east of my arbitrary dividing line are a motley linguistic family, and there has never been the strict social stratification of the West. China is a society without strata, more like a network, according to Professor Nakao Sasuke, a cultural anthropologist and China specialist. Sun Yat-sen, the father of modern China, said that Chinese are like grains of sand. Tibet, on the western edge of the region, is controlled by a priesthood whose high status rivals that of a nobility. However, even the children of very poor parents can enter the clergy if they begin religious training at an early age. Promotion is based on talent and effort; merit generates social mobility. The exception in the East is Japan, which was ruled by a distinct military class for many centuries. A feudal social structure comparable to that of Western Europe made Japan atypical.

Professor Ishida Ei'ichirō has suggested three geographical boundaries for culture. He draws a line "from the Mediterranean to the Bosporus" because Europeans regard the area east of this line as "the East." If we look at the West from Japan and ask at what point we become conscious of the West, many Japanese would draw a boundary line between Burma and India, Ishida says. (A third line through the Tsushima Straits marks Japan's cultural sphere.) I have travelled many times from Japan to Europe and Africa. As the airliner crossed from Burma into India I always felt, "I am entering a different world now." On returning to Southeast Asia from Calcutta, too, I had a sense of relief, as if I had just stepped into my own cultural zone. The tone of societies west and east of the Indo-Burmese border is radically different.

Consider what happens when a motorist is stopped by a policeman for a traffic violation in the East and West. In Japan, the driver's attitude should not be casual or legalistic: "I'll pay a fine and that's the end of it." He must show the officer that "I know I did something wrong and I will never again break a traffic regulation." If you convey an impression of sincere repentance, the policeman may well let you go without a ticket. Not so in the West. Kawashima Takeyoshi, a legal scholar and professor emeritus of the University of Tokyo, described an experience on a West German highway when a policeman pulled him over for driving too close to the car ahead.

Partly as an experiment, he said, he apologized to the German officer the way he would have in Japan. But it didn't work: he had to pay a fine. The policeman was very polite, however, handing over a receipt with a cheery, "Have a good trip, professor." In Japan, police officers treat offenders with stiff superiority; a casual comment is beneath their dignity. Yet the person who honestly admits his mistake and apologizes often receives only a warning. In the United States, if a motorist objects, "I didn't run the red light," the policeman will probably say in a businesslike way, "You just tell that to the judge in traffic court."

Traffic regulations have been strictly enforced in Singapore in recent years. Police stop drivers for minor offenses, but reportedly, as one might expect in an Oriental country, the contrite and deferential motorist is let off with a stern lecture. Generally speaking, in the West it is a losing proposition to admit you were at fault and apologize. In the East, it is usually more effective to express regrets to the other party by suggesting you were in the wrong. Western businessmen and visitors would do well to remember this when something goes awry in a commercial relationship in Asia.

That said, however, it must be noted that in recent years Japanese negotiating with foreigners—especially with Europeans, Americans, and Arabs—tend to use a Western-style assertiveness. Many Japanese executives have found from personal experience that they must be aggressive or put themselves at a severe disadvantage.

In the West, particularly in Europe, there is a series of disparate cultural spheres with many shared values and similar institutions. Western Europe can be regarded as a single cultural zone, for example. But in the East, cultural diversity rather than coherence is the rule. We generalize about "Western-style management" but no one would say "Eastern-style management." Experts like Herman Kahn correctly predicted that the countries deeply influenced by Confucianism would be the next region to industrialize. But there are enormous differences among Japan, South Korea, and the other newly industrializing countries (NICs) in the way groups or institutions are structured and function. Decision-making in South Korea, for example, tends, like that in China, to be centralized, with authority concentrated at the top. The reverse is true in Japan, where a popular consensus percolates up from below to become the national will.

Individualism and Birthdays; Groupism and Hot Baths

In Japanese society the organization is more important than its members. The group is the source of ultimate values, the loci of moral obligation. Western individualism celebrates a person's birthday as a special occasion. The date is marked by cards, flowers, gifts, and parties. To miss the date is tantamount to forgetting the person. But Japanese attach little significance to birthdays. Traditionally, the family assembled on New Year's Day and collectively congratulated one another on the passage of another year. The family as a whole was a year older; the particular day its members entered the world was not important. After World War II, however, the Western practice of celebrating birthdays spread to Japan and the old custom faded away. Nowadays Japanese children are delighted when an adult says "Happy Birthday" because it means they will get a gift. But after reaching the age when gifts stop, we tend to forget about our own birth dates.

Westerners like to name ships and streets after famous people—military heroes, politicians, and entertainers. South Koreans, being an individualistic people, also dedicate public places to kings and soldiers. But Japanese, with our emphasis on group effort, virtually never honor an individual this way. Occasionally an emperor's name is used on a vessel or road, but this really commemorates the era when he reigned rather than the sovereign himself. During the wave of Westernization that swept Japan in the late nineteenth century, many statues of famous men were erected in plazas and parks, but the practice stopped after World War II. The collectivity is important; there is no point in singling out one member for recognition.

The Western emphasis on the individual or the particular seems strange to Orientals, especially to Japanese. In the West a person's given or personal name is written before the family name. Letters are also addressed by house number, street, city, and state—from the smallest administrative unit to the largest. Yet the normal procedure for classifying anything is from the largest category to the smallest, i.e., from the whole to the parts. By reversing this order, Westerners show the primacy of the individual. With the exception of *Homo sapiens*, in nature the survival of the species is the most important imperative. The Japanese sense of priorities accords with the biological imperative and may explain how this country has survived.

In Japanese society, individual rights were always equated with private interests, which are inferior to public interests. The individual is *watakushi* (私), the personal pronoun "I," which also means "private" or "personal." Its antonym, *ōyake* (公) means "public," "the common good," or "the group as a whole." Although "private" has a favorable connotation in the West, *watakushi* has a negative implication vis-à-vis *ōyake*, the greater good. A standard dictionary defines *watakushi* as "(1) For one's own convenience; (2) to seek one's own interest; (3) selfishness; self-interest." The word *shishin* (私心), a compound of the characters for "I" and "heart," means that a person is selfish or motivated by personal interest. It is a virtue to sacrifice *watakushi* for the sake of *ōyake*. In this sense, *ōyake* is equivalent to *ie*.

Over the centuries Japanese have disciplined themselves to fuse the particular with the whole. Customs encourage group awareness. The Western bathtub is for individual use, for example. With the Japanese public bath (*sentō*) or the bath at a hot-spring resort, many people enter the same steamy water. Individuals cannot make selfish demands such as "I like the water hot" or "I prefer it lukewarm." All members of a group strip and bathe together, an intimacy—"skinship"—that deepens friendship.

When Japanese eat as a group in a restaurant, everybody usually orders the same meal. This unanimity strengthens group solidarity. I have seen the headwaiter in a French airport restaurant throw up his arms in consternation when every person in a Japanese tour group ordered exactly the same meal. To the independent French, with their love of personalized cooking for the discerning palate, our attitude toward food was barbarous, proof that we were totally devoid of individuality. Yet a Christian communion service symbolizes unity with a God who transcends the congregation. Japanese do not make a covenant with an absolute God. Instead, we value group solidarity, a social contract between intimates—company or community. Choosing the same meal shows a collective identity.

Chapter Five

The Roots of Japanese-style Management

The *sui generis* Japanese group seems to have been formed over many centuries in the benign isolation and mild climate of the archipelago. Continuous residence on these islands since antiquity has shaped a strong attachment to one's home town, or *furusato*.

Public opinion pollsters have found an unusual indication of this sentiment. Respondents to questionnaires bear down harder on their pencils or pens when filling in the space for home town than in the sections for age, previous jobs, etc. A home town is not necessarily where one was born. To a Japanese male now living in Tokyo, for example, it is where his father was born, the place he identifies with because his ancestors lived there for centuries. Japanese want to be buried in that same soil, to be united after death with their forebears.

The surprise attack on Pearl Harbor on December 7, 1941 (December 8 in Japan), sank many U.S. warships. All were subsequently refloated except the battleship *Arizona*, which remains a silent vestige of that Sunday morning. Each day the ship's flag is raised on the mast that protrudes above the water. Almost 50 years later, the remains of 1,177 crew members are still inside the capsized vessel. Thousands of U.S. soldiers killed in the Korean War rest in cemeteries in South Korea. Americans have no objection to overseas burial of their servicemen. But no matter what the difficulty or expense, Japanese want the remains of war dead recovered and interred in their ancestral graves.

The Imperial Navy battleship *Mutsu* sank in Hiroshima Bay after an accidental explosion in 1943. After the end of World War II it was refloated at enormous cost, and the crew's remains were recovered and cremated, then presented to relatives. Japanese family members of war dead would never leave them in another country. They want the remains brought home, as the fallen soldiers themselves would have wished. In June 1986, for example, the remains of three Japanese World War II prisoners were discovered at Fort Riley, Kansas. At the request of their families, the remains were exhumed, cremated, and returned to Japan.

This passion for burial in one's own land reflects the mindset of a sedentary agricultural people. If the Japanese were the descendants of nomads or immigrants, we probably would not have this intense attachment to our native soil. This powerful longing to be united forever with our ancestors, to sleep eternally under the same mountains and sun, is a distinctive feature of Japanese groupism. The group extends beyond contemporary associates to people of the past. The family encompasses lineal ancestors, and the company includes the founder and earlier generations of workers as well as present staff members.

The past is not gone forever but still lives on in the present. Remote ancestors or the dead founders of a company, in the form of *kami* or *sorei*, watch over their descendants or firms from the grave. Just as Christians pray to God for divine protection, Japanese appeal to their ancestors' spirits for divine intercession.

The *sorei* is an important key to understanding the Japanese way of thinking. Although no universal religion sprang up in Japan like those faiths from the desert or cold regions that worship an absolute God, the moderate climate inspired an animism that venerates the land and nature. From the late nineteenth century Japan's militaristic government systematically organized these beliefs into a nationalistic State Shinto. However, a primitive animism existed long before this modern manipulation. From ancient times this system of beliefs permeated Japanese spiritual and material life.

Many Japanese treat a paper talisman from the Ise Shrine, the holiest symbol of former State Shinto, as a silly superstition and toss it in the trash basket. But every family safeguards its Buddhist memorial tablets, a symbol of the *sorei*. In 1984 a volcano erupted on Miyakejima, an island in Tokyo Bay about 200 kilometers south of the capital, and many residents hastily fled from the burning lava. On television news broadcasts, several were quoted as saying, "All I managed to save were the ancestral tablets and our bank book." This is a typical attitude.

Surveys of religious beliefs show that even many Japanese Christians celebrate the animistic *bon* festival each August. Such data show that the belief in *sorei* is stronger than formal religion. A U.S. soft-drink company tried to exploit this sentiment one *bon* season. The Japanese-language edition of *Reader's Digest* carried a strange advertisement in the worst imaginable taste: "Pepsi Cola tastes so good your dead relatives will come out of the grave to drink it." This gruesome phrasing has all the markings of a third-rate American cultural anthropologist moonlighting as a copywriter.

South Koreans are more conscious of their family lines and maintain much stronger family ties than Japanese, yet they are an individualistic people. Koreans often say, "One on one, we can beat the Japanese. But if three-man teams from each country are pitted against each other, the Japanese always win." Although this is said in jest, Koreans are often good at individual effort and the Japanese excel at group action. For centuries Korea was a staunchly Confucian country, in some ways of a stricter persuasion than China itself. In recent years the number of Christians in South Korea has increased, to a reported 25 percent of the population. Christianity spread partly because of the fertile soil of individualism. The Korean family (*munjung* [門中], a compound made from the characters for "gate" and "middle") is led by the most capable or prestigious male. In the Japanese family (*kazoku* [家族], a compound formed from "house" [*ie*] and "family," or "relatives"), the eldest son almost automatically represents the family. Among agricultural peoples leadership positions were usually hereditary; among the nomadic peoples of northern Asia, however, ability was the criterion for leadership. A village head had little direct effect on the community's destiny, but an incompetent tribal chief could mean disaster; outstanding leadership was a life-or-death matter for nomadic tribes.

Japanese and Koreans may share a common ancestry, but the latter still show traces of the equestrian or cattle-raising culture of Northwest Asia. Japanese seem to be a mixture of northern and southern stock, but with the outlook of an agricultural people from the south.

Paddy Cultivation—The Hub of Japanese Culture

Paddy cultivation is the fundamental determinant of Japanese culture. It is the hub around which everything else, from alpha to omega, turns, according to Professor Ishida Ei'ichirō, whose ideas I have previously cited. The rice-culture region stretches across the monsoon belt. From Southeast Asia—Malaysia, Thailand, Vietnam, and Indonesia—it extends west to Assam, India, south to New Guinea, and east to South China, Japan, and the southern half of the Korean peninsula. As methods of rice cultivation improved—with new varieties, more efficient irrigation, and better paddy layout—demand rose with population increases. New areas were opened to cultivation in the twentieth century: Hokkaido, Manchuria, North China, North America, and parts of Africa.

In rice-growing regions life has been organized around the labor process. Many of the ceremonies and festivals of farm life stem from rice cultivation, as does animism. The moist soil and climate of paddy-field rice areas have greatly influenced national character. In outlook and behavior, the peoples who grow lowland, irrigated rice are exactly the opposite of peoples in arid, desert regions and quite different from wheat-growing societies.

In isolated Japan, villages developed six distinctive features that shaped our society and values. First, rice growing is a group endeavor. This is a crucial point. The *mura*'s work is decided by the group as a whole. Farmers work so close to one another that cooperation becomes second nature. There is nothing like the Kansas or Iowa farmer tilling fields miles from his closest neighbor. When paddy fields are irrigated—water pumped in or allowed to flow by gravity—the entire village's fields must be watered at the same time. Fertilizer applied to an upstream field seeps into the land of other farmers below; everyone has to use the same kind. Upstream farmers have to be very careful when they flood their fields or the paddies farther downstream will be completely submerged. The fields are drained as the rice approaches maturity, and everyone must do it at the same time.

Second, a wet-field rice society does not have a specialized division of labor. Hunting breaks down naturally into separate tasks: beaters flush the prey and attackers lie in wait for the fleeing animals. In the paddies, everyone is a generalist who must do all the tasks: prepare the land, plant, irrigate, weed, and harvest. Except for the physically infirm, collective community work does not allow individuals to choose their chores. These old agricultural work practices are the basic reason Japanese corporations use generalists instead of specialists. Management still believes that everybody should be able to perform all aspects of an operation.

A third feature of rice cultivation is repetition: every year farmers do the same hard work over again. There is none of the variety of hunting or a nomadic life. An animal who survives a trap or hunt learns from the close call; hunters must devise new stratagems. If, for example, an animal avoids a pit, then the hunters will try to flush it into the open where their bows and arrows will be effective. Matching wits with their prey, the hunters try new methods and weapons.

Even the fire-field agriculture practiced in mountainous parts of Southeast Asia does not entail the same monotonous tasks year after year: farmers change seeds and crops annually. But in paddy-field rice growing there is little variation from year to year. No drastically new methods can be implemented.

Weather is a variable factor, of course. Drought may reduce crop volume, but farmers can only use the same methods the next year and hope for rain. Japanese proverbs express the requisite stoicism: "Patience is the first virtue" (*Nanigoto mo shinbō ga daiichi*) and "Perseverance prevails" (*Ishi no ue nimo sannen*). The philosophy of many white-collar employees in large companies or organizations in Japan is based on a rural metaphor: if you patiently stay in one place, the crop will ripen and the harvest will be ample. They prefer lifetime employment with one organization and regular promotion through seniority, in contrast to their counterparts in the United States, where corporate head-hunting is a cottage industry and job-hopping is acceptable if not the norm.

A Chinese fable comes to mind. A peasant named Shou Zhu lived in the state of Zong (Honan Province) during the Warring States Period (402–221 B.C.). One day he was working in the fields and surprised a rabbit. The startled animal ran headfirst into a tree stump and killed itself. Thinking he had found a new means of livelihood, Shou Zhu gave up farming and watched the tree stump daily. In China, Shou Zhu, whose name means "to defend a job or slot," symbolizes the dimwitted rustic, and his name has become synonymous with one who forgoes effort and counts on chance success. It also stands for a person who, judging everything from the narrow outlook of very limited experience, cannot adjust to new situations. But if Shou Zhu had been a rice-growing farmer in Japan, his name would be synonymous with perseverance, the major virtue in success.

In World War II, the Japanese military repeatedly used the same tactics. If an attack failed, they launched another one exactly the same way. American officers reportedly were puzzled by Japanese failure to learn from past mistakes. My guess is that the rice-farmer mindset led them to repeat the same methods over and over again. Most army staff officers were from the peasant class, and they probably believed that at some point perseverance would succeed.

Imitating: Technology Transfer in a Rice-paddy Culture

A fourth characteristic of a rice culture helps to explain the oft-heard charge that "Japanese are good at imitating." Japanese companies are criticized for frequently copying foreign technology and products. But a paddy-field people naturally imitates a neighbor's successful techniques. Hunting is an individual activity, and the know-how can be kept secret. Rice is grown on irrigated plains, out in the open in full view of the community. Innovations are accessible to everyone. They cannot be hidden or copyrighted as intellectual property. A Japanese tour group's unanimity when ordering food stems from the same impulse to copy one's neighbors. It is as if a silent alarm sounds in each psyche: "Get in line!" The descendants of a hunting people, in contrast, all order differently. This is a hunter's psychology. In the JKC Businessmen Survey we asked: "According to one way of thinking, to exploit the results of another person's (company's) creativity and effort—to get a so-called free ride—is an acceptable, shrewd business practice as long as your action does not financially harm the other party. Another viewpoint holds that it is improper to utilize another company's asset regardless of whether it causes them financial loss. With which opinion do you agree?"

Table 7. Respondents who considered a "free ride" an acceptable business practice

Japan	66.5%
Korea (South)	54.2%

The ratio of Japanese respondents who conditionally approved a "free ride" was higher than for South Koreans. By age, the youngest Japanese (20–29) had the highest approval rate of 75.6 percent. Younger Japanese are the quickest to take advantage of a windfall situation. Although more South Koreans than Japanese say they are opposed to a "free ride," in fact the copying of trademarks/logos and production of imitations is a more serious problem in South Korea than in Japan. Ethical principles and actual business conduct often diverge.

In the West, where a "free ride" is considered unethical behavior, the approval rate would be low. The Sony candy case of the mid-1960s, in which I was involved, showed how tolerant Japanese society is of clever imitation. A small confectionery maker named a new hard-candy product "Sony," using the electronic giant's trade name without permission. It also copied Sony's vermilion package color and cartoon character. Sony filed suit for infringement of commercial rights.

The candy company's defense was: "We admit using the Sony name. However, we have not hurt Sony at all. They are a consumer-electronics manufacturer and do not make candy; our action has not reduced Sony's sales. Furthermore, the candy is a superior product, so Sony's trade name has not been damaged. Sony must prove it has been harmed."

This was a valid defense under Japanese law at the time (the practice was illegal in many Western countries). A free ride was only improper if it hurt the other party. Sony tried to show it had suffered financial loss. Eventually, there was a compromise and the suit was withdrawn—a typical Japanese solution. Much of the economic friction between Japan and the United States and the European Economic Community arises from fundamentally different perceptions of what is "fair." In the ancient rice culture of Japan, to quickly imitate and adopt a neighbor's skillful methods, far from being immoral, was considered a virtue.

Diligence, the merit of constant toil, is a fifth legacy of rice cultivation. The Japanese work ethic predates the transmission from China of Confucianism, which reinforced native industriousness. In a tropical area with abundant water, like the Assam region of India, farmers still use the original kind of paddy. By contrast, Japanese rice production became very sophisticated over the centuries. Farmers steadily improved their fields, giving them the same loving care that skilled craftsmen lavish on a work of art. Farm families worked hard in the slack season, too, weaving bags and ropes from rice straw. This diligence and exquisite workmanship underlie Japan's precision-machine industry today. Unfortunately, mechanization after World War II has largely deprived farmers of the discipline of physical labor.

A sixth feature of Japan's rice culture is a leadership style. Farm work, although a community enterprise, did not require a powerful, charismatic leader. The same operations were patiently repeated year after year in the same soil, and by much the same methods. The entire operation could be managed through unanimous village consensus without strong individual leadership. When the rice crop was safely in, the community would hold a harvest festival at the shrine. Even today, with agriculture completely mechanized, every village holds a harvest festival. The community expresses its thanks to the deities of heaven, earth, and rivers who provided the bounty. Often a popular elder who has worked hard on *mura* ceremonial events over the years is honored by being placed in charge of the festival. He is the event coordinator, another aspect of Japanese group leadership and decision-making.

Isolation and Social Classes

Geographical isolation had profound consequences. The military energy—the drive for conquest and plunder—that was a dynamic force on the Eurasian continent was almost always checked at the Korean peninsula before it could reach the Japanese archipelago. The great majority of the inhabitants of these islands since the dawn of history were never forced to flee their native place or conquered. Social classes and castes are formed when a society consists of conquerors and a subjugated people. Thus, classes in the Western sense did not develop in Japan. Of course, there were social strata like the nobility, samurai, and farmers. But there were never enormous disparities, such as that between a tyrannical king and a lowly slave; nor were status barriers immutable. Japan's homogeneity made unnecessary the severe sanctions found in countries riven by ethnic and class hatred. When two samurai groups fought, in most instances only the leaders of the defeated side were required to commit ritual suicide. Rank-and-file members of the losing camp were incorporated into the victorious *ie*. Desperate conditions provoked many peasant uprisings in Japan, but comparative research on agrarian revolts indicates that peasants in the West suffered incomparably harsher oppression.

Only in our bloody religious wars were large numbers of the defeated mercilessly slaughtered. The death of a leader and his generals did not suffice: masses of ordinary soldiers were also put to death. An uprising by followers of the Jōdo Shin sect of Buddhism in 1579 was suppressed by Oda Nobunaga (1534–82), an outstanding military commander who had conquered many daimyo and reunified central Japan. A harsh and mercurial man, Oda had the entire sect butchered. The Shimabara Uprising (1637–38) was a revolt of peasants professing Christianity, which the Tokugawa shogunate had banned. When the besieged Hara Castle on the Shimabara Peninsula, Nagasaki Prefecture, finally fell, every rebel was killed, including women and children. A total of 37,000 people reportedly died in the massacre.

Religious fanaticism has often led to bloodbaths in monotheistic Christian and Islamic countries, but Japanese have rarely turned the sword on each other for doctrinal reasons. There have been very few ruthless holy wars in Buddhist societies because the teachings of nonresistance and nonviolence mitigate sectarian intolerance.

Japan was on the brink of civil war in the spring of 1868 as the Tokugawa armies and units loyal to Emperor Meiji from the Satsuma and Choshu fiefs squared off for a showdown. But after scattered fighting, the leaders negotiated a settlement. They shared a sense of national crisis: "For Japanese to fight among ourselves when foreigners threaten the country would simply play into their hands!" The transition from the Tokugawa shogunate to the Meiji imperial government was handled like a family or clan dispute.

Japanese today feel the same way about foreign economic penetration. Rather than allow large U.S. or European corporations into the market, Japanese executives in a threatened industry prefer to form a united front against the intruders.

Competition in a Hot-spring Society

Spared the bloody struggles that raged across the Eurasian continent, Japanese enjoyed an insouciant communal life, much like a group of close friends relaxing at a hot spring. Until about a hundred years ago there was no Japanese word for "competition." Fukuzawa Yukichi (1835–1901), a famous writer and educator, coined the word *kyōsō* (competition) from two Chinese characters that mean "compete" or "contest." Fukuzawa explained that it was a very cutthroat Western concept. Was there nothing corresponding to economic competition in Japan until Fukuzawa made up the word? Of course there was, but the rules were as different as those of sumo and boxing.

Rough-and-tumble Western competition is guided by certain principles or conditions. Each participant has rights. Opponents contend rationally in a public arena, i.e., the free marketplace. The winner and loser can be objectively determined, and the loser departs with good grace. The confrontation is reminiscent of a European duel in which the swordsman who draws first blood is the victor. His opponent acknowledges defeat and withdraws.

A Western-style transaction is based on the rights of atomistic individuals. Buyer and seller engage in a no-holds-barred tussle in the marketplace. The seller uses all his leverage to get the highest price and the buyer bargains tenaciously to get the lowest price. Let's call this Rule 1. The struggle establishes a minimum-maximum point for both sides—the deal—and a clear winner and loser. If the vanquished party later strengthens his position, he can challenge the victor to a return match.

In Japan, the seller and buyer operate under a very different code. They both maneuver carefully so there will be neither a winner nor a loser. Both parties figure out the other's intentions, find a median point where each can make a profit, and conclude the deal at that price. I call this Rule 2. Westerners see this as a form of collusion.

Japanese find Rule 1 conduct ruthless and follow Rule 2 to avoid disrupting a communal society. Within the Japanese economic milieu, Rule 2 works effectively; to outsiders like the U.S. government and American corporations, however, this must look like a closed community obstructing free-market forces. This perception gap is a major reason why foreigners think the Japanese market is closed.

Much of Japanese business is organized into corporate groups (*keiretsu*) centered on banks. For example, manufacturer A-1, general trading company A-2, and hotel A-3 belong to Bank A's group. Japanese find it perfectly logical that hotel A-3 should offer discounts to companies A-1 and A-2. Some American economists call this discounting unfair because the corporate group is a giant, closed network. For manufacturer A-1 to purchase only from general trading company A-2 is clearly discriminatory, they say. These economists argue that in an equitable system, manufacturer A-1 allows a trading company from corporate group B to bid publicly for its business. By the same logic, the Nippon Telegraph and Telephone Company's (NTT) practice of purchasing products only from the family of domestic makers was labeled unjust. The United States insisted that NTT should allow American companies to compete fairly for its business under Rule 1 (i.e., competitive public tenders). U.S. industry became strong by companies fighting and destroying each other; they insist that Rule 1 apply in every situation.

Americans believe that unless there is a marketplace, as defined by Rule 1, the situation is inherently unfair. This has encouraged "whistle-blowing"—reporting on misdeeds by superiors—in the conviction that disclosure of corporate misbehavior like price-fixing helps to root out corruption and improve society. Whether such conduct is moral or not ultimately boils down to culturally determined ethics. In China, Korea, and Japan, Confucianism taught that to report a person to whom one is morally obligated, especially a parent (even if the father or mother had committed a crime), was reprehensible behavior no matter what the apparent justification.

Long isolation might have helped to fashion Japanese society into a community with strong spiritual bonds. Japanese tend to regard their work organization as a fictive community, or family, and to identify with it totally. What is good—profitable—for the company is also proper and appropriate. Strong loyalty to the group overrides abstract civic obligations. Not many Japanese would quibble with Charles E. Wilson's famous dictum that "what is good for General Motors is good for the country."

In the United States, corporate raiders acquire a company by buying up its stock. However, in Japan a hostile takeover by stock purchase is regarded as unethical because a corporate merger links two human communities, not two sets of paper shares. A U.S. corporation is owned by the shareholders; a Japanese company is a community, from management to employees. Taking over another firm is equivalent to seizing another village by force.

When Sumitomo Bank, one of Japan's largest, tried in the mid-1970s to acquire, by legal methods, a small, local bank in Osaka, David fought Goliath and appealed to public opinion. In the end, Sumitomo abandoned the takeover bid and got only a reputation for roguish behavior.

In the United States, joint research by two companies can be considered collusive conduct, a restraint on trade, and evil because it harms third parties (Rule 1). In Japan it is perfectly proper for the Ministry of International Trade and Industry, acting as an intermediary, to organize and assist private corporations in collaborative research and development. In a communal society like Japan, cooperation is *wa* (harmony) and perfectly legitimate, another facet of Rule 2. Japanese emphasis on collective effort runs counter to the American/European preference for individualism.

Anthropologists do not make value judgments about behavioral differences. Cultural relativism precludes calling either groupism or individualism superior. But we can safely say that American negotiating and analytical methods, and South Korea's also, are rational. By contrast, there is a singularly emotional aspect to Japanese ways.

The Korean commentator O-Young Lee, in his book *Small Is Better: Japan's Mastery of the Miniature*, cites a famous legend to show the illogical dimension of Japanese thought and negotiating tactics. Part of Japan's creation myth, the incident is recorded in the *Kojiki* (Record of Ancient Matters). According to the account, Susano-o, the younger brother of Amaterasu, the Sun Goddess, committed many antisocial acts. Amaterasu became angry and hid in the Rock-cave of Heaven. The world became pitch black and many bad things happened in the darkness. Community members were very upset and planned to lure Amaterasu out of the cave so the sun would shine on the world. The method they hit upon was to assemble people in front of the cave, light a fire, and have Ame no Uzume, a skilled dancer, perform in front of the fire. The girl's mimic dance was very interesting, and the amused crowd laughed uproariously. Thinking that the show outside must be worth seeing, Amaterasu opened the cave door a little and peeked out. In that instant the powerful Ta-Jikara-o opened the cave door wide and dragged Amaterasu outside. Once again the world was in light.

Lee says that Japanese methods were devious. If this had happened to Koreans, the community would first have assembled in front of the cave and tried to negotiate with Amaterasu logically: "Susano-o's behavior was wrong, but staying in the cave because of it harms all of us. We will make Susano-o mend his ways, and we want you to come out." This is the rational way to persuade a recalcitrant goddess, Lee says, but the Japanese used a trick to get Amaterasu out of the cave. Instead of reasoning together, they chose deception and duplicity. Lee concludes that Koreans have always been bamboozled by Japanese chicanery.

Given Japan's record in Korea, Lee's ire is understandable. Foreigners often see Japanese tactics as cunning or crafty. However, we consider such methods not tricky but ingenious. There was no need for logical or so-called fair methods of bargaining and competition in Japan's communal society. Amaterasu, deceived by the *mura*'s trick, came out of the cave smiling wryly. The Sun Goddess realized that she could not continue to inconvenience the entire *mura* because of personal pique, so she overlooked their subterfuge. The *Kojiki* compilers considered the social context—the feelings of both sides in the dispute—when they approvingly included this story.

Clusters of Competition

Japanese-style competition is between clusters. Here I am using "cluster" in its technical sense. In statistics, when total sets of elements are classified into groups, as far as possible each group is composed of homogeneous elements and is itself heterogeneous. The separation of the entire set into groups is called stratification, and each group forms a stratum. Conversely, the internal elements of each group are, as far as possible, heterogeneous, and each group is homogeneous. Separating the total set into groups is called clusterization, and each group forms a cluster.

Competition among clusters characterized Japan's military forces up to the end of World War II. The Imperial Army should have handled land operations, with the Imperial Navy responsible for sea warfare. They should have cooperated to accomplish national objectives, but bitter interservice rivalry consistently marred military operations. The Imperial Army and Navy had their own air forces. (The U.S. Army and Navy also had separate air forces, but they worked well together.) The navy developed the famous Zero fighter and the army built its own Hayabusa (Falcon) fighter, an inferior aircraft. The navy refused to provide Zero technology to the army. Neither air wing ever standardized parts or attempted to share technology.

It was often impossible for the Imperial Army and Navy to conduct combined operations. On Saipan, where the Japanese garrison was virtually wiped out when U.S. forces captured the island in 1944, there were two separate command structures right up to the end of the fighting. One army staff officer wrote in his diary: "Before we can fight the Americans, we have to waste time and energy negotiating with the navy for supplies. It's a shameful situation."

Because of the navy's uncooperativeness, the army wanted its own maritime forces. The generals began building a cargo-carrying submarine and an aircraft carrier (a converted commercial vessel) for army use. Not to be outdone, the navy formed its own ground unit, a Marine Corps. The Imperial Army did not utilize navy personnel in designing the submarine. Even if the generals had asked, the admirals surely would have said no. At the final stage, however, the army ran into problems beyond its technological grasp and reportedly swallowed its pride and requested navy assistance.

Throughout the Pacific War the army and navy operated as separate military commands, each with its own land, sea, and air arms. Japan's military organization consisted of two disparate clusters that were never stratified into a planning and command structure.

Business competition in Japan is among industrial groups similarly arranged in clusters, such as the Mitsubishi group and the Sumitomo group. These clusters consist of heterogeneous elements grouped around a major bank—a general trading company, steel maker, machinery manufacturer, electronics firm, and a petrochemical producer. Within a cluster, personnel exchanges are relatively easy. An official from Fuji Bank may be put on the board of directors of a company in its group. But personnel rarely if ever move between groups. It is not unusual for a director of Mitsubishi Corporation, a trading company, to be placed on the board of Nippon Kokan K.K., the giant steel maker, which also belongs to the Mitsubishi Bank group. But a Mitsubishi Corporation executive would never go to Mitsui and Co., which is also a trading company but in a different group.

Major universities in Japan are also self-contained clusters. Graduates of the most prestigious universities will almost never be offered teaching positions at universities other than their own alma maters.

The rivalry among clusters or between two companies in the same cluster is very different from competition in the United States. Each cluster corresponds to a large *mura* or *ie*. As in the Imperial Army and Navy, each *ie* is self-sufficient in highly trained personnel. If a cluster needs people with special skills, for example software engineers, they rarely recruit from another cluster, particularly not from one with which there is a strong rivalry. Just as the Imperial Army built its own submarine, each cluster usually develops its own capabilities. This is another reason Japanese companies prefer to train their employees as generalists.

Japanese society is like a self-sufficient cluster. Although the complex world economy requires an international division of labor, Japan retains an across-the-board manufacturing capacity. The refusal to hire non-Japanese personnel—foreign factory workers or executives—is another attempt to maintain these pure clusters.

A strong sense of rivalry toward other countries pervades Japanese society. An island people long accustomed to peace and security, we are particularly apprehensive about threats from abroad. We have no place to flee; we must stand and fight. On several occasions, Japan has fought off foreign attackers with extraordinary national unity. In the centuries between these rare crises, however, this island Shangri-la enjoyed peace, and the arts and letters flourished. The late Heian period of the tenth and eleventh centuries and the Genroku era in the early eighteenth century are thought of as cultural golden ages.

A Culture of Special Integrity

Geographical isolation combined with a homogeneous population, formed into distinct clusters and imbued with an intense sense of solidarity, produced a culture of special integrity. Our culture retained its original identity despite an extraordinary degree of cross-fertilization. The result was a hybrid culture able to accept things foreign and preserve unique indigenous elements. The Japanese still enthusiastically adopt words from other languages; there is nothing like the French attempt to exclude foreign loan words in the name of linguistic purity. Japanese think borrowing enriches a language; the French and Koreans fear it mongrelizes their mother tongue. At the same time, however, although Japanese have long been receptive to foreign influence, they have always staunchly defended their original culture. To draw a botanical analogy, Japanese culture is like a hybrid plant formed by cross-fertilization with many species but which has never lost its original character. This is what I mean by a special integrity.

Japan has absorbed and assimilated everything from the Chinese writing system to parliamentary democracy and the assembly line. This voracious appetite for foreign culture is aided by a powerful enzyme process that digests the alien fare. Certain aspects of advanced civilizations have been accepted even though they conflicted with the existing culture. Buddhist images were first transmitted to Japan from the Korean peninsula in the mid-sixth century, triggering a debate at the Imperial Court over whether Japanese should worship the Buddha. The Mononobe family argued that to worship a foreign god would offend the ancient deities. The Soga family countered that all the peoples to the west worshipped this god; for only Japanese to reject Buddha defied common sense. Soga-no-Iruka, whose attitude toward foreign culture was classically eclectic, prevailed. Japanese gradually put a local stamp on Buddhism by retaining the animistic belief in *sorei*. In the middle ages each Shintō shrine also revered a local Buddha (*honchibutsu*). These were Buddhas who were reborn as original Japanese gods (or Japanese gods reborn as Buddhas). Buddhist deities were incorporated into a belief in indigenous *kami*.

Catholic missionaries brought Christianity to Japan in

the sixteenth century. They thought Japanese would quickly accept the faith, but they knew what had befallen Buddhism: one Spanish missionary reported that Christianity itself might be transformed before it could sweep the country. The priests feared that Christ, like the Buddha, might become a local deity, a *honchi-Christ.* Missionaries had succeeded elsewhere by purging native gods as idols; they failed when an indigenous faith like Islam was too strong. But in Japan the danger was that the Christian God would become a prisoner, naturalized into the local spirit world.

Once a Buddha or the Christian God, or even the Greek pantheon for that matter, are in the fold of Japan's communal society and mingle with its other deities, they are accorded equal standing. The Seven Gods of Good Fortune have been venerated in Japan since the tenth century. They include Ebisu, an indigenous *kami*; Jurōjin, the Old Man of Long Life, a Taoist figure from China; and Bishamon, a Hindu god. Our attitude is, "If they bring luck and happiness, then their country of origin is no impediment to enshrinement." The Japanese are spiritually omnivorous.

We have equally catholic tastes in food. Television cooking programs show the enormous interest in foreign cuisine; ordinary families eat dishes from the West, China, or Korea several times a week. Although Americans may dine out at a Chinese restaurant or Japanese sushi bar, at home they rarely prepare Oriental foods. Chinese and Korean friends tell me that they eat Western steak or Japanese tempura in restaurants, but at home they eat only native food. Japanese cooks are gradually naturalizing overseas cuisine, much like the blending of alien religion with local beliefs. *Tonkatsu*, for example, is a Japanese version of a pork cutlet, and *ramen* is a kind of Chinese noodle. Japanese life is not being Westernized or internationalized; foreign things are Japanized and then take their place in our homes or stomachs. This is equally true of ideas about business and management: they are gradually altered as they enter our commercial life.

The Roots of Japanese-style Management

We have seen that the early Japanese, isolated from the Eurasian continent, lived in small villages organized around cooperative work in rice farming. The prototype of contemporary Japanese groupism was the *mura*, a self-contained community whose members, all of roughly equal status, toiled diligently year after year at the same communal tasks.

Continental influences entered the archipelago like an intravenous injection: slowly, gradually, drop by drop. Over the centuries Japanese society developed an antibody to alien influence. This robust culture bent foreign things into new, compatible shapes, never losing its own identity.

From ancient times, Japanese residences had a hanging bamboo screen, a *misu*, in the entranceway that enabled occupants to see outside while they themselves were shielded from view. Similarly, our forefathers watched developments in the outer world from behind the protective veil of isolation and adopted or copied other civilizations. It was a one-way flow: foreign culture entered but nothing went out. Japan remained a mystery, even its name uncertain to Marco Polo who called it Zipangu, Zipangii, Cyampagu, and Cimpagu.

Japan brought foreign legal and political institutions inside the screen. In the seventh century the imperial government adopted T'ang China's legal code and administrative structure; in the late nineteenth century the Meiji government repeated the process, this time borrowing parliamentary institutions from Europe. The borrowing was always highly selective: alien institutions were modified to fit current needs. Japanese are about the only non-

Western people with a democratic, parliamentary system.

After World War II, Japanese business leaders turned avidly to the United States for inspiration. The list of borrowings is long: the division system of company organization in which each division manufactures a separate line of products, the matrix organizational structure, strategies for overseas operations, product-planning methods, quality control, marketing techniques, and, most recently, the concept of venture capital. Japan sought models in the United States and copied them en masse.

Yet a close examination of these transplanted foreign models, from the political party system to stockholder-centered capitalism, shows that the Japanese versions were pseudo copies. Western labor unions, for example, in Japan became not craft- or industry-wide organizations but enterprise-based unions, i.e., at the company level (in each *ie* or cluster). The U.S. line-and-staff system was altered: the staff withered, its functions performed by line units. Again, we see clusterization. Although Japanese studied U.S. management strategy and decision-making and adopted the terminology, the extent to which these concepts are being used in their original sense is problematical. The form was taken but the substance was altered. To put it positively, the prototypes were skillfully modified to meet local realities. The best known example of reshaping U.S. ideas to Japanese patterns is quality control. In Japan, QC was initially linked to small-group activity in the workplace and then broadened into a total quality control (TQC) movement. It became an integral function of manufacturing, eventually spreading to other sectors of the economy. U.S. marketing techniques were another hot import. In the early 1950s, American specialists were invited to Japan to lecture or were hired as consultants. There was no Japanese word for "marketing" until this time. One of the lessons learned helped greatly to accelerate economic growth: make products for segmented markets. Automobiles for export meet different specifications depending on the destination: vehicles have left- or right-hand drive, and their paint and weather-resistant protection vary according to exposure to sand storms or saltwater corrosion. Again, we see a cultural enzyme at work digesting foreign ideas.

Japan's culture and organizational style did not grow endogenously. There was cross-breeding with other societies, but the original form—the "Japaneseness"—was preserved. What about the future? Will Japan continue its insatiable adoption of foreign ideas while retaining its own distinctive way of doing things? Today we face two new problems. One is that the seedbed of overseas creativity is withering; new species suitable for cross-breeding seem to have disappeared. The second is that in the past Japan brought alien ideas and goods inside the *misu* but let nothing out. Now we must make our culture available to other countries. Ironically, it is the one product we have no experience in exporting.

Chapter Six

Communication

The way people queue up for a bus or wait in front of a public building shows attitudes toward space. In Japan's gregarious culture, the distance between people in a line is very short; everyone seems to be all scrunched together. When Westerners, with their strong sense of individuality, line up, the interval between them is fairly wide. They seem to abhor being packed cheek to jowl with strangers, the daily routine for millions of commuters in Japan. Westerners dislike direct physical contact with people they do not know. Yet when there is some degree of intimacy, they shake hands, and both men and women embrace members of the same sex in public. Physical contact verifies friendship. In Japan, even very close acquaintances do not express familiarity by touching and holding.

Generally speaking, individual Westerners maintain a wide space around themselves. In private homes each person tends to have his or her own room. Japanese families live as a group in small rooms. Residential land is expensive and houses are small, of course, making some degree of crowding inevitable, but actually we prefer to live close together. Since ancient times there has been no significant trend toward larger houses.

In Europe and the United States, until a few years ago, public telephones were in individual booths. In Japan, most public telephones are not enclosed: there are rows of phones on counters outside railroad stations or at department store entrances. Japanese regard the telephone and the bath as a public areas, and we do not mind sharing them with others; Westerners prefer privacy in both. Railroads are another example. In the West, private compartments are popular, but in Japan travelers have never wanted such accommodations.

Office space per white-collar employee in Western corporations is almost twice that in Japanese firms. Executive-level offices are exceptions, but normally in a government agency or company many desks face each other in a large room, and the clerks work amidst the general hubbub. In Western companies, even junior staff members have their own offices or work two to a room; in some U.S. corporations each employee has his or her own work space.

Space utilization corresponds to the organizational ethos. In a Western corporation, each employee is responsible for work assigned by a superior. When the job is done, the employee goes home, even if a co-worker is still busy. But in Japan, because white-collar employees cooperate and share tasks, an individual rarely works overtime alone. The spatial placement of everyone together in a large open area has encouraged colleagues to help each other.

Each culture establishes fixed distances between people when they communicate or interact. Americans want about 1.5 meters between themselves and the other party during a conversation, and Latin Americans stand less than one meter apart. A North American talking to a Latin American feels some anxiety because the other person gets so close. Japanese also prefer about a 1.5-meter distance from the other party when speaking. We do not gesture while talking; it is considered unrefined.

Egalitarian Groupism

Japanese society is like a large room undivided by partitions or screens. Friends in a *mura* live comfortably without privacy. In this sense, Japan is a classless society. Is a preference for an unstratified society unique? The Japanese manufacturer YKK built a large factory in Liverpool, England. One job involved very noisy operations. The usual solution in the United Kingdom is to enclose that employee's work site, to protect others from unnecessary noise, and pay the employee extra for the discomfort involved. But the Japanese managers thought it inhumane to isolate one employee in a small room. Believing it better for all the workers to endure some of the noise and share the inconvenience, they used the large open-room layout and did not partition off the one workplace. British workers agreed to the arrangement.

A major feature of Japanese organizations is an egalitarianism that, as far as possible, treats all members the same. Western companies usually have separate dining facilities for managers and ordinary workers. In Japan, except for the most senior executives, company cafeterias are not segregated. Despite sharp status distinctions in Europe, Japanese companies there have used common eating rooms with favorable results. The egalitarian, fraternal management methods established in Japan after World War II seem to have worldwide applicability. (They are more popular with mid- and lower-level workers than with executives in overseas firms, however.)

Prewar Japanese management was hierarchical, because of the vestiges of classes from the feudal period and the system of nobility and status distinctions adapted from the

West after the Meiji Restoration. Several years ago I visited a factory in Pusan, South Korea. Although the wide main gate was open, workers were pushing and shoving through a small side entrance. I asked why employees were not allowed to use the main gate. My guide said it was reserved for management, a practice Koreans had inherited from the Japanese colonial period. This conversation reminded me that in the teachers' lavatory in my elementary school, the urinal farthest to the right bore a notice: "For the principal's use only." Old Japan was not egalitarian.

The prewar Japanese National Railways had first-, second-, and third-class cars. There were separate waiting rooms and ticket wickets for each class of service. Today Japan's is the world's only major rail system, including those of the socialist countries, with a nominally single-class service.[1]

"Social equality" or "leveling" may be better terms for Japan's single-class culture than egalitarianism, which is associated with the "*egalité*" of the French Revolution's slogan of "*Liberté, egalité, fraternité.*" "*Egalité*" is equivalent to equal human rights. Japan's social equality is closer to *fraternité*, a kind of middle-class togetherness. Everyone—the elite and the masses, the rich and the poor—is regarded as the same.

In Chapter 5 I noted that Asia never had rigidly stratified societies like those of the West. Many of the class divisions found among Caucasoid peoples are based on lineages, esteemed or denigrated, that can be traced back to the ancient relationships of conquerors and conquered or of original settlers and later arrivals. The upper and lower

[1] Long-distance express trains on Japan's newly privatized Japan Railways have so-called Green Cars, which are equipped with more comfortable seats and are more expensive than regular cars. However, JR does not officially consider Green Car service as First Class; commuter trains and most short-distance trains do not have Green Cars. First Class and Second Class cars were abolished twenty years ago.

strata frequently have different physiques and facial features. In Britain the top strata of politicians, business executives, military officers, and religious leaders come from the nobility or gentry, and in the United States they are white Anglo-Saxon Protestants (WASPs). Families with distinguished bloodlines, imbued with a confident sense of ruling class privilege, lead these societies. Some typical families are Nelson, Wellington, and Roosevelt. They take the initiative and assume leadership positions in organizations. In Asia, with a few exceptions, there has been very little dominant control by a few distinguished lineages. This is true of Japan also, mainly because since historical times the population has not been conquered by another ethnic group; no permanent ruling class was ever formed. After World War II, a democratic ideology from the United States entered this relatively fluid society. In addition, economic recovery and affluence enabled all members of the *mura* to have a middle-class lifestyle. Social equality is now the norm.

Visitors and Hospitality

Factory visits allow an outsider to glimpse national character. In West Germany, visitors are unfailingly offered coffee. If the tour runs into lunchtime, the guests are invited to eat in the executive dining room. Next to each item on the menu is its caloric content, a splendid touch of German efficiency. At most French factories, however, visitors are not invited to dine and usually are not served coffee.

It is not that Germans are more hospitable than the French, nor that the latter stint on amenities. The extremely individualistic French consider dining a personal matter. Eating with affable companions in a carefully chosen restaurant is the essence of the civilized life. French managers probably feel that since they do not know the observers' food preferences, both sides should refrain from suggesting that they dine together. The same attitude presumably applies to coffee as well.

In Japan, no matter what the occasion, guests are served green tea. Cafeterias provide it without charge. The word *mucha* (unreasonable) consists of the characters for "not existing" (無) and tea (茶). Not to offer a visitor even a cup of green tea would clearly be "unreasonable" behavior. Japanese have made sipping the beverage an aesthetic ritual—the tea ceremony—and several schools teach "the way of tea."

In China, visitors are always served hot tea in a lidded cup, and refills are plentiful. The Chinese invented the tea house and consider the beverage a catalyst for social interaction. Further to the west, in Bhutan, everyone carries a wooden bowl inside the upper garment. At a host's invitation, it is taken out to accept tea with butter. In every cultural region, a cup of tea brews communication.

The custom of drinking tea has been declining in South Korea in recent years. The Confucian rulers of the Yi dynasty opposed tea because it was introduced by Buddhist monks. (Ironically, Confucianism was a greater force in Korea than in China, its wellspring.)

Communication begins with the first contact. Consider the following situation. A meeting has been arranged between companies A and B. Each is represented by three men—a director, general manager, and section chief, all of whom must be introduced to each other. Would you start from the ranking person—the director—or from the section chief? Westerners say they would introduce the senior person first. Japanese start from the junior person and proceed to the senior. Although some people may not follow this practice today, because of Western influence, in ancient times formal contact between two groups in Japan began with the lowest-ranking members stating their names and positions. This is still the practice in sumo and the martial arts, where tournament matches start with the junior ranks.

A Japanese tends to defer to someone whose status or accomplishments are unknown. Upon learning that the other party is lower in rank or younger in age—i.e., not someone who need be taken seriously—the Japanese abruptly becomes arrogant. In my experience, Americans tend to do just the opposite: they initially assume their status is higher. If it turns out that the other person is more distinguished, the American apologizes and then acts deferentially. In the initial stage of a relationship, a Briton will suddenly ask a probing question and watch the reaction. A sophisticated, witty response wins the other person a "good-chap" rating and cordial treatment.

Each society has a distinctive etiquette for first contacts. Japanese instantly whip out a name card that shows their organization and position. Some foreigners who have done their homework now also immediately present a name card. This effort to understand the other side's customs is crucial in negotiations or collaborative work between groups from dissimilar cultures. A disaster story will illustrate the point.

A Japanese company and a West German firm were considering a tie-up. Preliminary discussions were promising, and negotiating teams from each corporation met to hammer out a basic agreement. Throughout the meetings the senior Japanese representative sat straight in his seat, said nothing, and often closed his eyes. Angered by this apparently aloof indifference, the German team finally broke off the talks. All the careful spadework and planning was wasted. Later, the Japanese side reviewed the situation and apologized, but the Germans were not mollified. Yet if they had understood local customs better, the negotiations would not have collapsed. The senior Japanese representative's function in such talks is to keep the agenda moving and make the closing statement. When he is satisfied with the course of a discussion, the leader usually just listens to what his younger colleagues are doing and says as little as possible himself. In the meeting with the West Germans, he sat silently with his eyes shut, like a Zen monk practicing meditation, precisely because the talks were going well. He was unaware that Westerners expect the highest-ranking person to be in charge, personally asserting his authority with comments like "Smith, you're the expert on this. Please explain it."

In Noh plays or classical dramas where Japanese gods appear, the lowest-ranking deity comes on first and the most prestigious last. In the West, usually the most powerful god appears first, a sign of primacy and leadership; the lesser gods follow later. In traditional Japan, when a new project or issue arose in a village community, lower-ranking or junior people usually discussed it among themselves first. After they had reached a general understanding, the matter was referred up the seniority ladder until the elders made the final decision. Foreign business executives who deal with government offices should not assume that "if we talk to the man at the top, everything will be O.K." Everything should be cleared with the junior staff first. In Japanese society, the lowest working level has important discretionary authority. Without a compelling reason, senior people cannot override the decisions of subordinates.

Leadership Styles

I do not mean to suggest that subordinates are ignorant of or indifferent to the preferences of people above them in the hierarchy, or that they make all the decisions and just pass them up the chain of command for formal ratification. On the contrary, low-ranking individuals always try to assess the probable response of those at the top. They ask, "If I were in their position and faced this problem, how would I handle it?" It is an attempt to anticipate intuitively another person's position before it is clearly articulated. There is constant communication, formal and informal, between superiors and subordinates to ensure that they are both on the same attitudinal wavelength. Co-workers drink and socialize together after office hours because a steady exchange of ideas is essential.

This organizational process—the orderly transfer of information and opinion from subordinates to seniors—is why reaching a decision is tortuously slow but implementation is rapid. When the senior person gives the green light, those who will actually do the work are fully prepared to move. They have been in on the decision and done the preliminary research and coordination. In China and the Arab world, Japanese businessmen have often found that a top official approves a project but nothing happens. When subordinates are asked how the matter stands, they say, "My boss may have promised you that, but I haven't heard anything about it from him."

Traditionally, as we have seen, Japanese generals remained at the rear where they could the monitor the battlefield and judge their officers' tactics and fighting skills. This style of leadership allowed subordinates to show their mettle; the top commander had to be a person of great character who would reward them fairly and overlook minor mistakes. There were also Japanese military men who led their forces by personal example, like Horatio Nelson and Alexander the Great. Minamoto Yoshitsune (1159–89) and Oda Nobunaga both died in battle, their dreams of national unification unfulfilled. To reach the pinnacle of political life or become head of a large organization in Japan, a person must be perceived by *mura* members as kind, generous, and broad-minded, capable of thinking of the interests of the whole group. These qualities are more important than personal bravery or vigorous direct leadership.

It is exciting to serve under dynamic leaders like Minamoto Yoshitsune and Oda Nobunaga (or their corporate equivalents); but when such leaders are cut down, their subordinates' chances for fame and fortune die with them. Brilliant generals such as Takigawa Kazumasa and Akechi Mitsuhide would have had even more distinguished careers under someone other than Oda Nobunaga. A would-be leader in Japanese society cannot be aggressive in the American style. In a baseball game, the pitcher is the focus of action but the catcher directs the whole team. No matter how brilliant the hurler, he needs a steady, experienced receiver behind the plate who can call the pitches and plays. In a *mura*-like organization where everyone knows each other, the person who pushes his own candidacy is far less likely to be chosen to head the group than a modest, circumspect individual.

An orchestra conductor directs from in front, the classical position of a Western leader. In a traditional Japanese ensemble, the leader is inconspicuous, on the end of the last row of musicians. Westerners may wonder how he can "conduct" from there, but it is the perfect spot for Japanese-style leadership. When Japan's communal groups are organized like an *ie*, there is high-context interaction (to borrow Hall's term), and members create harmony by tacit understanding. Each musician pays close attention to the movement and sound of those nearby. From the rear, the conductor can see if the group is functioning well together. All Japanese learn this technique; it comes with the culture.

Our school system teaches students not to disturb group order. Morishima Michio, professor of economics at London University, in his book *Nihon to Igirisu* (*Japan and Britain*), cites the Suzuki method of teaching young children to play the violin as an example of this socialization. Conceived by Shin'ichi Suzuki, the technique assumes all children have talent that can be developed by early training.

According to Morishima, this approach reflects Japanese education's emphasis on raising the average level of the group. Teachers try to bring the class up to the 80 level rather than have a few students score 95 and the rest be in the 70s. According to Morishima, when Suzuki pupils realize that they have played a bad note, they stop briefly, correct themselves, and then resume playing without upsetting overall harmony. British children are the solo type. In a similar situation, British youngsters ignore how others are playing and continue in their own way. The whole group may soon be playing at different tempos unless a strong conductor controls the anarchy. This skill at unobtrusive mid-course correction is why Japanese orchestras can always attain a respectable level of performance, above average but not outstanding, says Morishima.

In the West a symphony orchestra, baseball team, or corporation is an assemblage of individual stars; their Japanese counterparts are composed of group-minded team players. Not surprisingly, the leadership is also different. In the West competition is between strong personalities, and an individual must actively lead or others will not follow. In Japan group harmony comes first. Followers are relatively docile, but the leader must be skillfully unassertive. Contemporary Japanese education, particularly compulsory schooling through ninth grade, is largely responsible for this unique group culture. Students are not regarded as individual personalities but as a collective mass.

Although this approach has a long history in Japan, it became pronounced after World War II with the growth of the mass media and the reduction of social differences. My early childhood education, for example, was not nearly as conformist as schooling is today, a point which Professor Morishima also makes. Many talented individuals who grew up in the prewar period escaped the snare of higher education. People like Matsushita Kōnosuke, founder of the Matsushita Electric Industrial Company, and former prime minister Tanaka Kakuei went to work at an early age and developed strong personal styles. A surprising number of well-known Japanese scholars—anthropologist Nakane Chie, historian Etō Shinkichi, economist Okita Saburō, and others—spent their childhood abroad in Manchuria or China. They seem to be a different breed from the average person reared in this isolated, peaceful society.

The outcome of individual combat and group conflict, in war or in business competition, is decided by different criteria. In a one-on-one contest, the stronger or more skillful person triumphs; in a contest between groups, other factors come into play, such as friendship among group members and willingness to sacrifice for the organization. A Japanese adage says "the victor is also the virtuous," i.e., only by being virtuous can a person win. Success is attributed to spiritual rather than physical qualities. Most Japanese believe that an individual or group triumphs because of moral superiority. The losing group was not just inferior in strength; it failed to create *wa* (harmony). Its members were deficient in group morality. Thus the winner also scored an ethical triumph. Since ancient times the victor in Japan was automatically regarded as legitimate and morally just.[2]

Nemawashi

The function of a meeting or conference in a Japanese group explains certain distinctive features of decision-making.

Shiba Ryōtarō, a well-known writer of historical novels,

[2] A Korean friend disputes this equation of victory and virtue, objecting that sometimes even the person whose cause is just loses because of physical or material weakness. For obvious historical reasons—Korea's loss of its independence and annexation by Japan in 1910—South Koreans believe that defeat does not tarnish a valid cause.

has described an early attempt at a Western-style meeting. The scene was a conference of prefectural governors held at the Honganji temple in Tokyo's Asakusa section. The meeting was inspired by the first article of the Emperor Meiji's Charter Oath of April 1868: "Deliberative assemblies shall be widely established and all matters decided by public discussion." Kido Takayoshi (1835–77), a powerful leader of the new regime, presided. Lasting a month, the conference was supposed to be the forerunner of a popularly elected assembly. But to Japan's ruling class, the Western practice of deciding matters at an open meeting seemed absurd. According to the memoirs of Shionoya Ryōkan, vice-governor of Aomori Prefecture, "most of those present showed their contempt for the proceedings by sleeping during the sessions, snoring loudly, or yawning in boredom." Only the staff and a few others took their duties seriously. Shiba comments, "One reason for the farcical situation was that Japanese were not accustomed to Western-style meetings. Also, they may not have had the stamina to sit through long sessions. Most important, however, was that nearly all the participants were contemptuous of the concept of decision-making at an open meeting. When asked to raise the right hand to signify approval or the left hand to indicate rejection of a proposal, Ōyama Tsunayoshi, governor of Satsuma Prefecture, raised both hands. Kido said, 'You cannot raise both hands. Are you in favor or opposed?' Ōyama smiled ironically and said, 'Either way is all right.' "

Open conferences or public meetings to decide important matters were rare in Japan. Of course, *mura* members got together to discuss village business. But it was not the practice for representatives, without prior consultation, to meet in a hall, debate issues openly, and make policy. That is still not the Japanese way.

Japanese talk over important matters in small groups or

use the *nemawashi* process ("binding the roots") whereby one person consults all the interested parties in advance. The meeting held when *nemawashi* is completed is a ceremony to approve publicly the decision reached beforehand. Not all meetings are mere confirmation rituals, of course, but the more significant the occasion, the stronger its ceremonial character. Important meetings take very little time. General shareholders' meetings, for example, end in a few minutes.[3] The serious exchanges between stockholders and management about corporate earnings and policy that often occur in the United States are the exception in Japan. The government revised the Commercial Law in 1982 to make shareholders' meetings more like the U.S. model.

To nineteenth-century Japanese, accustomed to *nemawashi* and behind-the-scenes decision-making, Western-style meetings must have been a shock. Commodore Matthew C. Perry and Townsend Harris, the first American consul, had great difficulty negotiating with Japanese. Their diaries and other records show that both men were often infuriated at the vague, vacillating replies of officials. Frustrated by meetings that were largely taken up by ceremonies or where the main topic was never discussed, they said the Japanese were slippery as eels. But Japanese were inexperienced in dealing with people from a different culture. We are still not skillful at diplomatic negotiations or working with foreigners in a joint venture. The director who sat like a Zen monk throughout the talks with a West German company was a textbook example of this lack of know-how.

In the JKC Businessmen's Survey we asked the following questions:

[3] Many corporations pay professional stockholders, called *sōkaiya*, who usually have connections with organized crime, so as to prevent hostile questions and expedite meetings.

> Should a matter affecting all members of the organization be decided by formal, open discussion? Or is it better to first obtain an informal consensus?
>
> In decision-making, should time be spent on open discussion or should it be utilized for preliminary *nemawashi*?

Significantly more Japanese than Koreans approved of the informal decision-making method, another indication that South Korean organizational behavior is closer to the American pattern than to the Japanese.

High Context, Low Context

Japan consists of groups of homogeneous people who speak a common language and share a long historical experience. Within a group there are few confrontations or serious differences over basic issues. Because they think alike, Japanese groups have high-context communication (see Chapter 4). As Edward Hall noted, few social rules are stated, and a great deal must be filled in with the imagination. In America's multiracial society, with its great variety of ethnic life-styles, religious affiliations, and attitudes, communication is often low-context. Hall compares it to "interacting with a computer—if the information is not explicitly stated, and the program followed religiously, the meaning is distorted." Japan was a closed, stable society for so long that Japanese have been culturally trained to understand each other intuitively, by mutual sensitivity, even without verbal communication. By contrast, the heterogenous American population lives in a low-context milieu where, if messages are not explicit, clear, and logical, communication often breaks down.

Haiku, the seventeen-syllable form of poetry, developed in Japan because of the society's highly contextual human relationships. Unless both the composer and reader of haiku have a common background and emotional makeup, communication via such concise verse would be impossible. Conversely, learning to write and appreciate this allusive, disciplined poetic genre trains people for in-group membership. The Japanese group is sympathetic and congenial, very sensitive to signals and stimuli.

Westerners usually negotiate in an adversarial relationship. Both sides bring certain advantages to the table, and bargaining is the process of sorting out and objectively measuring demands. When Japanese negotiate among themselves, it is taken for granted that both parties will show concern for the other and be willing to compromise: "I have made this concession so I know you'll make one too."

Sincerity

For historical reasons, Japanese are not experienced in objective analysis of their own motives or position vis-à-vis others. We often stubbornly insist on impractical demands or, at the other extreme, make unnecessary concessions. Especially when negotiating with strangers, many Japanese do not objectively evaluate their strengths, weaknesses, and objectives. Instead, the basic approach is to present yourself as "sincere" (*seijitsu*). It is a technique to show that one has no ulterior motives, that you have good intentions and are serious about the mutual interest involved in the project or deal. *Seijitsu* and its oft-used synonym, *makoto*, are often translated as "honesty," "faithfulness," or "singlehearted." They are akin to the Zen mental attitude of the mind as clear as the purest water or purged of any egoistic or selfish motive. Actually, *seijitsu* is an extremely subjective, self-satisfying ethic. If each side did not have "selfish motives," what would there be to negotiate? Nevertheless, Japanese have usually believed that if they discussed an issue "sincerely," the other party would see their "sincerity" and respond affirmatively.

Japanese often do not carefully plan bargaining tactics and lack the detachment to see that negotiations are a kind of game. Instead, we try to convey a "sincere" attitude and show we are "free of guile or deceit." When the other party does not reciprocate or the project collapses, as frequently happens, frustrated Japanese ask themselves, "I was totally sincere, so why did I fail?" We love to use words like *wa* and *makoto* as slogans. Most companies and private residences have calligraphy, either a scroll or framed inscription, in which the characters for *wa* and *makoto* are drawn in bold strokes. *Makoto* was the central concept in the Emperor Meiji's Imperial Rescript to Soldiers and Sailors (1882), a fascinating source on traditional values. Five virtues essential to soldiers are listed: loyalty, respect, valor, faithfulness, and simplicity. Then they are all distilled into *makoto*.

> These five articles should not be disregarded even for a moment by soldiers and sailors. Now for putting them into practice, the all important thing is sincerity. These five articles are the soul of our soldiers and sailors, and sincerity is the soul of these articles. If the heart be not sincere, words and deeds, however good, are all mere outward show and can avail of nothing. If only the heart be sincere, anything can be accomplished.[4]

[4] *Makoto* and *seijitsu* are among the Confucian virtues. However, *seijitsu* was an ancillary moral quality in early Confucian doctrine and not stressed in orthodox teachings in China and Korea. It became a central virtue in Japan during the Tokugawa period, particularly through the work of the Confucian scholar Itō Jinsai (1627–1705). Itō insisted that in all things man must use objective reason or logic *and* subjective human feelings, and *makoto* was an important element of the latter. *Makoto* is a common given name, the virtue becoming, nominally at least, an integral part of the person.

The person with *makoto* has a sense of moral rectitude; those who lack it or whose conduct falls short of this criterion feel guilt. But once this virtue is extrapolated from the individual level to the realm of diplomacy or international business, it becomes extreme self-righteousness. Other people are puzzled and annoyed, and the technique may backfire. Professor Sagara Tōru, who taught the history of Japanese ethics at the University of Tokyo for many years, has written in *Nihonjin no kokoro* (*Japanese Values*) that the greatest task facing Japanese today is to rid ourselves of this self-righteous moral concept of *seijitsu*.

Family suicides in which one or both parents kill their children and then themselves are fairly common in Japan, though rare in the West and elsewhere in Asia. This apparently bizarre act can be explained by the *seijitsu* virtue. According to Professor Sagara, family suicide is acceptable in Japan not because Japanese believe it is all right to kill family members if the household is in desperate financial or emotional distress; rather, parents who love their children consider it morally correct to force kindness on them, so the children are killed to spare them hardship. If this subjective feeling of *seijitsu* is all we need to live in this society, according to Professor Sagara, life is very simple and Japanese have nothing to learn from other countries.

Seijitsu is a faithfulness to good intentions. In 1985, a Japanese woman living in California, despondent over her husband's infidelity, attempted to drown their two children and herself. The children died, but she was rescued and survived. Although she was originally charged with murder, U.S. authorities decided that the act stemmed from her cultural background, and the charge was reduced to voluntary manslaughter. The woman's feelings of *makoto*—that death was the proper choice under the unbearable circumstances—were understood by the American prosecutors and judge.

Transplanting *Nemawashi*

Unlike the attitude of *seijitsu* or *makoto*, the *nemawashi* technique has international applicability. Americans have recently recognized its utility in some kinds of cross-cultural negotiations. When a deadlock occurs at an international conference, for example, frequently a brief recess is called. Away from the official bargaining table, the parties reach an understanding. Then they return to the formal setting and ratify the arrangement.

Other countries have words similar to *nemawashi*. In English there is "lobbying;" Filipinos say, in Tagalog, *barangai*; and Indonesians have *mushawara*. But the connotation of each is a little different from *nemawashi*. With "lobbying," the objective is crucial; with *nemawashi*, the process itself is the main point. Everyone gets the satisfaction of having participated behind the scenes. Even if some participants are not present when the final decision is made, each feels "I was kept informed of developments along the way." No one is disgruntled at being left out.

Bernard Krisher, former Tokyo bureau chief of *Newsweek* magazine, obtained an exclusive interview with Emperor Hirohito before His Majesty's visit to the United States in 1975. Krisher has written that he spent a year arranging the interview. Over several months he met with mid-level officials, about 50 persons altogether. Krisher explained the need for such an interview, asked that his request be kept confidential, and said he hoped they would not oppose the project when it came to their desks for comment. According to Krisher, success in dealing with Japanese requires a flexible approach tailored to the other person's status and situation. Timing is important, and you must wait for the right opportunity. He thinks Japanese tend to reach a consensus without exhaustively considering a matter. *Haragei*, or "belly play," the art of reading the other person's mind to reach an understanding without explicit statements, has certain advantages, says the journalist. When everyone understands each other's intentions, communication is very rapid. Although Japanese do not have rigid principles, according to Krisher, they have pride, a subjective personal honor (or "face"), which it is dangerous to ignore.

Slavic peoples, by contrast, are suspicious of informal negotiations away from the official conference table, according to Professor Hall, and they tend to be uncomfortable about such contacts. To Slavs, a meeting is a verbal battlefield where negotiators forcefully assert their positions and contend for advantages and concessions. Even experienced Western diplomats reportedly find it very difficult to negotiate with the Soviet Union. Indefatigable Soviet officials often prolong discussion until the other side is physically exhausted. Japanese are at a severe disadvantage in this kind of negotiating.

Hall cites Greeks as another people who have lower-context communications than Americans. However, Greeks do not regard a meeting as necessarily a process to reach a conclusion. Appreciative of the sharp exchange of ideas and of clever expostulation, they purposely seem to complicate the verbal give-and-take. The way people negotiate and what they expect from the venture reflects their cultural milieu and historical background.

It is standard business practice in Japan to intuit the feelings of the other party in commercial negotiations; it is usually possible when both parties are high-context Japanese. In the West, when a restaurant is not open for business, a "closed" sign is placed on the door or in the window. In Japan the sign says, "Preparations under way" (*junbichū*). The former is a one-sided announcement by management; the latter, with its promise that food will eventually be ready, shows concern for the feelings of the hungry, disappointed customers. Some especially considerate Japanese restaurant operators use a sign that says, "Please wait a little while."

Language sets the tone of a business transaction. Consider the initial exchanges in a Japanese and in a South Korean shop. A customer enters a small store and, finding it unattended, says rather loudly, "Is anyone here?" In Japan, the proprietor emerges from the living quarters at the back and says, "Welcome to my shop. What can I show you?" In South Korea, the shop owner replies, "Here I am." The Korean response is a logical rejoinder to the question. But Japanese greetings have nothing to do with logic. Warm, polite, and solicitous, they make the customer feel appreciated.

In negotiations between Japanese organizations or individuals, both sides strive to perceive and respond to the other party's feelings. People who can readily grasp each other's needs and objectives become friends. The person who cannot empathize is placed outside the circle of close associates. Among themselves Japanese ascertain from a few brief remarks whether the other party is a kindred soul, the kind with whom they can relate. Messages about education, status, social background, and political views are instantly transmitted and received. When common ground is recognized or both sides realize that with time rapport seems possible, then, even if they are in a fiercely competitive position, neither treats the other ruthlessly. Both parties try to establish a cooperative relationship. For example, when two businessmen are negotiating a deal, both will carefully prepare beforehand to figure out the other's position and find a point (price) that is mutually profitable. As Western economics textbooks show, however, the strategy of European or American businessmen is to drive the price up or down to the most profitable point, i.e., the lowest margin for the other side. The law of supply and demand, or mini-max theory, is their basic model. Western executives often say the Japanese way of accommodation is collusion. They think a "collusive" agreement is wrong because two separate, distinct parties are involved who should press for maximum advantage. This is the mind-set of individualism. But to Japanese, with their sense of collective identity, the Western method lacks consideration for the other party. Japanese organizations function through cognitive antenna alert to potential trouble. Members analyze how far a project, for example, can be pushed. To go too far or too fast may antagonize other players. The plan must be adjusted to the human environment. Ample care is taken not to embarrass colleagues in a meeting. When a person who is attuned to the human environment hears the first three ramifications of an idea, he or she should be able to anticipate the next seven. By fine-tuning this intuitive skill, usually organizations can deftly avoid or quickly resolve problems.

To cite an everyday example: two trucks approach each other in a narrow street. The drivers think there may be just enough room to inch past each other without scraping. Both truck drivers turn their steering wheels slightly away from the oncoming vehicle, carefully inching ahead. They maintain eye contact but neither says anything or even gives a hand signal. Each responds to the other truck's movement. First one advances and then the other. Each driver senses the other's reaction and turns his steering wheel in response.

Maneuvering through narrow streets and alleys is a trick all Japanese truck drivers and deliverymen learn. In my travels in Europe, North America, and Asia I have never seen anything to equal this nonverbal communication. Curiously, in those countries famed for articulateness and logic, drivers are less skilled at compromise and preserving undented fenders than Japanese truckers, who never say a word. This was brought home to me on a trip to India when I witnessed a confrontation between a bus and passenger car on a mountain road. If the bus had moved a little to the left, the car could have gotten through without going close to the dangerous edge of the cliff. But the bus driver refused to give ground. The automobile driver got out and approached the bus, and a long discussion ensued. Finally, the bus driver eased his vehicle over to the left slightly so the car could get by. But voluble negotiations were required.

Indians are extremely argumentative and logical. The study of logic as an intellectual discipline developed in India much earlier than in Europe; there was never a similar scholarly discipline like it in Japan.

Returning to the topic of meetings: in Japan the *nemawashi* process is essential, the actual meeting secondary. Then what is the function of a meeting?

According to textbooks on management, in order to survive, all organizations must (1) accomplish the objective for which they were established and (2) give their members a feeling of worthwhile participation. Thus, meetings help attain organizational goals by drawing out the opinions and information of participants and shaping them into a consensus. Because many people participate, meetings are also an effective motivational technique.

However, if an organization has a better means of collating information and involving employees, meetings are not so essential. Japanese companies and government agencies have diverse methods of communication and decision-making that perform many of the functions of formal meetings. They include *nemawashi*, conversation among staff in workplace groups such as quality control or project groups, and informal meetings. Although the *ringi* system is less used now, it is another method of communication. In this system, a lower-ranking employee or official drafts a proposal with supporting justification, and circulates it to others concerned with the matter. If superiors agree with the idea, they approve it by placing their seals on the document. This method is the approximate equivalent of a meeting.

Yet corporations and other organizations report that the number of meetings is increasing, and many people find themselves always in some kind of conference or session. Why are there so many meetings? One reason is that many organizations have become very large; the proliferation of committees and task forces indicates growth. Another factor is Western influence. There now seems to be a widespread perception that agreement in a meeting format is a necessary step in group decision-making. Even though a consensus has been reached informally by *nemawashi* or other methods, it must be formally authorized in a meeting. In many companies, the meetings of general shareholders and boards of directors are mere formalities. They are held simply because of a legal requirement; the important decisions have already been made elsewhere. Nevertheless, these meetings have become indispensable. They complete the process, much as a period unmistakably marks the end of a sentence.

Form and Substance

All societies, to a greater or lesser extent, skillfully distinguish between "form" (appearance) and "substance" (content). The expression "To say is one thing, to practice another," an English proverb I learned in middle school, illustrates that the gap between verbal commitment and implementation is universal. But in Japanese society the bifurcation of "ideal" and "actual" is particularly common. On the one hand there is *tatemae*, which has been defined as "surface phenomena" and "the formal public self . . .

ritualistic and preoccupied with status." On the other hand, there is *honne*, "what lies beneath" or "the private self . . . informal, warm, close, friendly, and egalitarian."

Another dichotomy is *sōron* (general principle) and *kakuron* (application). In the early 1980s, everyone agreed, for example, on the need for administrative reform of the Japanese government (*sōron*) but many fought particular changes (*kakuron*), especially when their special interests were threatened. Japanese think in terms of *omote* (the outside, what is shown/said to others)—the ideal—and *ura* (inside or behind)—the less-than-perfect actual. We accept these categories as natural law. Moreover, because we operate in a high-context environment, everyone usually knows exactly which is being used, whether to take a person literally (*honne*) or with many grains of salt.

Why do Japanese use concepts like *tatemae* and *honne* so much? Why do we shift back and forth constantly between form and substance? The divergence usually occurs when there is a clash between traditional and modern normative values or codes of conduct. When a country with its own centuries-old ethical norms and rules of behavior is forced by external pressure to adopt different values, as Japan was by the West in the nineteenth century, people are trapped between indigenous norms and modern ideas. They must accept Western values (humanism, individual rights) for appearances' sake—Japan would not have been regarded as a modern state otherwise—but they preserve the traditional norms in their everyday lives. They try to be true to both codes, since they want to be good Japanese and also enlightened, modern men and women.

The Second Party—*Nijikai*

Corporate communication and decision-making processes are not restricted to official meetings, of course. Social gatherings enable people to unwind from work pressures, encourage friendship, and maintain morale. In Japan the official meeting (*tatemae*) is followed by a party where people can be candid (*honne*). As a method of organizational communication, the later session ensures that new policies will be smoothly implemented. Decisions are usually by unanimous agreement, not by majority vote (see Chapter 2). Although no objections or dissent are expressed at a formal meeting when a course of action is ratified, there are always some members with strong objections who have been forced to go along. At the post-meeting party or get-together, the group leader placates the disgruntled minority. This effort to console an unhappy faction usually continues with a second party (*nijikai*) after the official party. A follow-up party is necessary because at the first affair, official rank distinctions obtain. The second stage is informal; fewer people are present, and all barriers of position or rank are discarded. In this relaxed atmosphere real communication takes place; everyone gets a bit drunk and talks freely. Statements that would never be uttered under normal circumstances are blurted out. Japanese society allows candor in a relaxed setting. *Mura* consensus-building takes place seriatim: *nemawashi* → official meeting → formal party → informal *nijikai*.

Avoiding Responsibility

The primary reason Japanese want to avoid formal meetings as a decision-making method is a dread of personal responsibility. Whether it is recognition of outstanding achievement or blame for failure, there is an aversion bordering on taboo to making a specific individual accountable. Policy is carefully made by the entire group. Once a decision is reached, unanimous consent is preferred over majority vote.

Before a formal meeting the participants reach an understanding which is then unanimously confirmed and approved. The result is the responsibility of all members collectively, not of a single individual. Even if an official record is kept of a meeting, it does not indicate who was really the prime mover in the group's action. After World War II, the Occupation tried to identify the main proponents of attacks on the United States and Great Britain in 1941. Investigators found that although none of the individuals in the key organizations enthusiastically advocated hostilities, they had all gone along with the group consensus. The participants all described a vague decision-making process, said they personally had not favored military action, and were unable to explain how it had happened. Strong leaders in Germany and Italy led their countries into the war. But the Tokyo War Crimes Trials never identified an individual who initiated the chain of events. This was not because the Japanese had covered up the facts. Top military and civilian officials plunged Japan into war by a process of collective responsibility (or collective irresponsibility). In Japanese society it is not individual will but group mood—"the way the wind is blowing," or the bandwagon effect—that moves organizations.

When peasants revolted in Tokugawa Japan, they signed a covenant with their names radiating from a center, instead of listed vertically by status or alphabetical order. If the document was made public, the authorities could not tell who the ringleaders were. There were no real leaders in peasant revolts, at least not in the Western sense of charismatic individuals who articulated agrarian grievances. All the village members helped to organize a protest; it was a collective decision, much like the way Japan went to war.

All participants are equal in a unanimous decision by group consensus. This equality probably originated in paddy-field agriculture. Farm villages did not hold public meetings and decide matters by a show of hands—"All those in favor, all those opposed"—with a simple majority the winner. Villagers first discussed issues in small groups and then collated these views into a conclusion by unanimous consent. This gradual, participatory process avoided bruised feelings and resentment. Furthermore, if something went wrong, there was no single person who could be blamed (or, alternatively, who got all the credit for success).

In old Japan, village leaders used *nemawashi*, meetings and persuasion to get everyone's approval for an action. *Mura* members understood full well that the leaders wanted a consensus, i.e., no dissent or disgruntled faction. At the *nemawashi* stage and later at public gatherings, villagers refrained from expressing strong views that might be divisive. Eschewing confrontation and not locking themselves into intransigent positions, they stated their opinions cautiously in an atmosphere of mutual forbearance. Feelers were put out, trial balloons launched. Little by little the dialogue advanced, no one playing all his cards at one time. The headman's job was to spot the points of unanimity.[5] The process had a happy ending when an area of agreement was found and a course of action emerged almost automatically. Then the chairman said, "Today, thanks to everyone's efforts, we have reached agreement on this matter," and bowed deeply to the participants. They also bowed to him and said, "Thank you for pulling everything together."

The vagueness of the Japanese language is a great asset. Differences of opinion are muted so the discussion can continue. We use the clause ending "*-desu ga . . .* ," equivalent to "but . . . ," to advocate a position and immediately give the opposing view. In short, everyone uses moderate lan-

[5] This is one reason why Japanese do not express firm personal opinions when asked to comment. They prefer to be part of a group consensus rather than assert an individual ego.

guage, acknowledging an alternative position (or an opponent's contention) as they go along. The dialogue advances an inch at a time, much like sappers clearing a mine field. Westerners trained in rhetoric prefer soaring leaps, but haste is equally risky in a mine field or in consensus-building.

Meeting participants do not demolish each other's arguments or attack another person's opinion. Instead, they move by accretion, with A's clarification added to B's original position, and then C's improved concept placed on the verbal pile. Finally, by a cumulative process, there is a conclusion to which all have contributed.

In mathematical terms, this method of discussion is like integral calculus; the Western style resembles differential calculus. The Western scientific method reaches the truth by rigorous analysis; Oriental philosophy finds the truth by synthesis. In mathematical terms, when two integers are given, a Westerner looks for the greatest common divisor, whereas a Japanese looks for the least common multiple. This can be illustrated with the mathematical set shown in Figure 5.

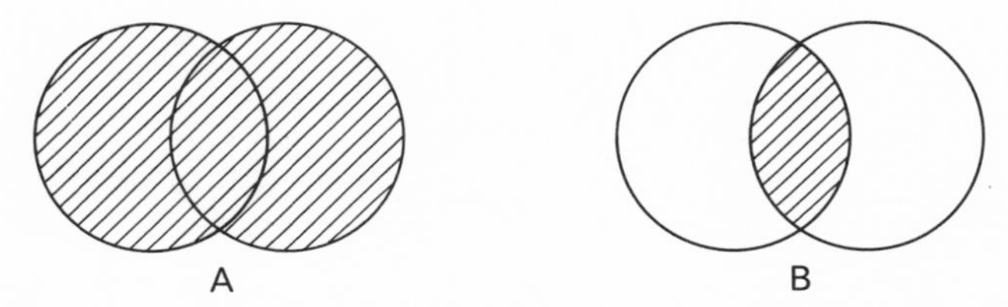

Figure 5. Reaching Conclusions, Japanese (A) and Western (B) Style

The left pair of circles (A) in the figure represents the way Japanese opinions are harmonized: the sum set integrates large elements of both. The circles on the right (B) show how Westerners adjust opinions: the product set (overlapping area) is corroborated by each party. As a mathematical term, the Japanese *wa* (harmony) also means the sum or total. Actually, harmony is the least common multiple supported by the members of a group.

When there are irreconcilable positions in a committee, for example, Japanese custom is to list them in the final report in parallel form. This indicates mutual respect for both sides. In a similar situation in the West, the conflicting views are not included in the final document. The opposing parties are satisfied that they did not compromise their position. They agree to disagree.

Japanese are often misunderstood or mistrusted in international negotiations because they never give a flat "no" or interpret the other side's negative response to their own position as an absolute rejection. A Western "yes" refers only to the overlapping part of the product set; the remainder on both sets is "no." But a Japanese "yes" covers the whole sum set; there is no "no" portion.

Chapter Seven

The Japanese Aesthetic Sense

The aesthetic sense of what is natural or beautiful varies enormously by country; even in one society, standards change markedly over time. Deep in the collective subconscious of Japanese is a sensitivity that shapes the behavior of our organizations and corporations.

Let us identify the distinctive aspects of Japanese aesthetics. Sen no Rikyū (1522–91) was tea master to the leaders Oda Nobunaga and Toyotomi Hideyoshi and founder of the Sen school of tea ceremony. One bright autumn day, having invited guests for a tea ceremony, he ordered a young monk to clean the small temple garden. The monk swept up every fallen leaf and told Rikyū that the job was finished. The tea master glanced at the scene and stepped down into the garden. He gently shook two or three trees until a few dead leaves fell to the ground. "Now the stage is set for our guests," he said. This is a refined Japanese sense of nature.

A South Korean intellectual has criticized this incident as typical Japanese affectation. A Chinese would probably have left the garden clear of leaves, as the priest had cleaned it, he said; and Koreans would have held the ceremony with all the fallen leaves just as they were, in their natural state, finding that truly beautiful.

Chinese prefer the artificial, and Koreans the untouched, while Japanese want the natural and artificial fused into a perfect harmony. These national differences are apparent in garden landscaping—the way trees and bushes are planted or stones arranged.

As the Rikyū anecdote indicates, Japanese carry artificial beauty to the extreme by recreating the epitome of nature. Bonsai, the dwarf trees that resemble large natural trees, are the classic example. Though they are shaped by human hands, no wild shrub looks so natural. Japanese bonsai enthusiasts work for decades and centuries—some plants are 500 years old—using every human technique to create a perfect miniature, the quintessence of a natural tree.

The result is a fusion of total artificiality and sublime naturalness. This philosophy of blending two dichotomous elements into a new harmony is not found in the West, China, or Korea. Westerners always distinguish man-made from natural and natural from artificial; there is a profound incompatibility.[1] Hegel even excluded nature and natural beauty from his *Aesthetics*.

Herbert A. Simon, the Nobel Prize-winning economist, was intrigued by Japanese aesthetics. In the Japanese edition of *The Sciences of the Artificial*, he wrote that Americans are deeply impressed with the way Japanese culture harmonizes human beings and man-made objects with the

[1] Landscape gardening in the West and Islamic countries is symmetrical, as in the main garden of Versailles. The design and shrubbery are extremely artificial; no plant ever grew in such shapes. Man conquers nature, which has been vanquished without a trace. Although Japanese landscape gardening has an enormous man-made dimension. great efforts are made to retain natural forms. The setting is so authentic that the untrained observer cannot identify human input; there is no sign of the gardener. Perfect effacement of the human effort is achieved with bonsai.

natural environment. Such skill and dedication are lavished on a bonsai that the viewer cannot tell where nature ends and artifice begins.

Scientists are now working on fifth-generation computers. Unlike the mechanistic and inorganic contemporary machines, computers of the future will be able to express human value judgments and emotions—love and hate, happiness and sorrow—a biological dimension. Japanese have a natural affinity for machines with human-like sensitivities. Workers name robots after popular female actresses and singers and regard them almost as human co-workers. Nature and man-made objects are viewed as coequal; machinery and equipment can be living objects akin to human beings. This anthropomorphism is central to the Shinto tradition. In the West, automation and industrial robots have often been seen as an alienating force; Japanese workers have never had this attitude. Unlike in Great Britain, there have been no strikes protesting the use of new machinery or factory automation. Japanese religion does not posit a dichotomy of man and machine, man and god, man-made and natural. There is no sharp distinction between living organisms and inanimate objects. Westerners name ships and buildings after famous people as a form of immortality. Japanese workers personify production machinery with the names of popular singers, as if they were giving a nickname to a co-worker; and a machine gains life. This unique way of interacting with nature and machinery is a distinctive aspect of Japanese culture.

Views of Nature: Macro, Intermediate, Micro

Professor Ueda Atsushi, of Osaka University, has classified human views of nature into macro, intermediate, and micro. He puts Western attitudes at both ends of the spectrum and Japan in the middle. According to Ueda, Westerners have contrasting attitudes. On the one hand, they speak reverently of the Himalayas and the universe (outer space) as overwhelming; on the other, they try to control and dominate the natural world. Westerners either have a sense of awe, almost worshipful, or they ruthlessly bring nature to heel. The Japanese middle way tries to befriend nature, seeing it as man's equal.

American conservation philosophy allows a forest fire in a national park caused by lightning to burn itself out. Wild animals must forage for themselves; park rangers do not feed them. U.S. conservationists believe that an ecological system sustained by man is no longer wild. This macro view respects nature and tries to preserve it unchanged. However, Americans also use whips and other kinds of discipline to train animals to be submissive. The way circus animals are turned into performers is the worst example. This is the micro attitude: creatures are broken to human will. There is a similar pattern in Western child-rearing methods. Children are forced to obey adults by threats and corporal punishment. In the days of the White Man's Burden, Caucasians used the same methods to subjugate Asians and Africans.

In the Japanese middle way, nature, animals, and young children are treated almost like friends, as putative members of the adult family. Animals and robots are assigned human characteristics; it is not an us–them or friend versus foe relationship. This attitude has shaped the methodology of Japanese zoologists and anthropologists. Western scholars, assuming that *Homo sapiens* is a higher species, use the outside-observer technique. Japanese zoologists, especially those at Kyoto University who study the behavior of anthropoid apes, use a participant-observer method. Researchers associate with the apes as equals, becoming part of the apes' ecology. The zoologists gradually learn the apes' language, and reportedly are accepted into the simian community. Inherent in the Japanese view of nature (or of man-made machinery) is a unified system in which the observer and the object are merged—scholar and ape, assembly-line worker and welding robot.

This fusion of subject (artist) and object of perception (scene) is characteristic of traditional Japanese painting. Since the Renaissance, Western artists have used perspective: objects in the distance are smaller than those in the foreground. The artist places himself in a certain spot outside the scene. From this stationary point the artist tries to view the object—a landscape—objectively. Japanese painters, however, draw proportions exactly as they are (i.e., the rear part of a building is the same height as the front) and shift their own perspective. The artist inserts himself into the scene. Even houses in the old *emakimono* were drawn like an unfolding diagram on which all parts can be seen (Figure 6).

In Western aesthetics, the artist first decides on his perspective and then focuses on the objective world. His will organizes the external reality. This is the standard Western approach to the world as object. The attitude toward organizations or human beings in formal theory, which is the mainstream of American management theory, is a classic

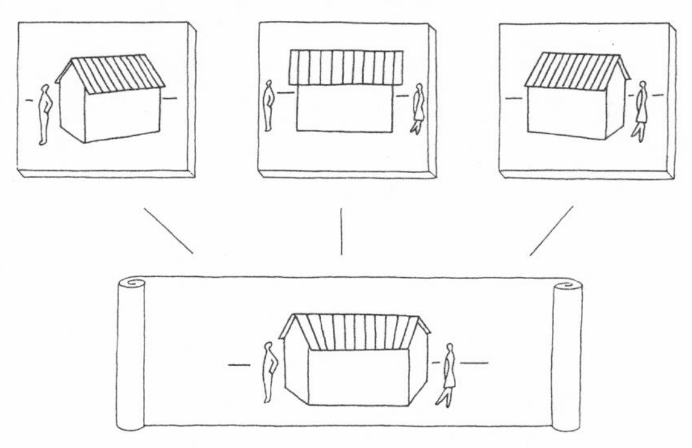

Figure 6. Artists' Perspectives.

example of this way of thinking. The entrepreneur or manager is the artist who occupies a fixed locus, and the employees correspond to the landscape.

The intermediate view of nature—accommodation instead of conflict—is often called typically Oriental, but many aspects are unique to Japan. Chinese and Koreans, for example, both put sugar on watermelons that are not naturally sweet enough, whereas Japanese add a little salt in the belief that this brings out the natural sweetness. A Korean laughingly quipped that Japanese make watermelon into *kimchi*, the traditional spicy side dish of Korea. But we do not heavily season a watermelon the way Koreans do cabbage for *kimchi*. Only a few grains of salt are sprinkled on. Just as Sen no Rikyū shook only a few dead leaves into the swept garden, there must be exactly the proper amount. The Japanese aesthetic sense is delicate.

We bring external objects like nature or machinery into the human world to make them part of ourselves, in much the same way that we accept foreign culture. This mindset has infused Japanese organizations since ancient times (and shapes management methods today). A distinctive, ubiquitous feature of Japanese culture is the attempt to merge and unify elements that Westerners distinguish sharply: god and man, animals and human beings, machines and workers.

To the Greeks, goodness, truth, and beauty, even in their highest form, remained distinct. In the Japanese mind, ultimately the three coalesce into one value which is often called simply "beauty" (*bi*). In this sense, beauty is the supreme value of Japanese culture. Westerners distinguish between the ideal of artistic beauty—"a lovely flower"—and the ethical ideal of virtue—"a good heart." But Japanese often say that someone has "a beautiful heart" (*utsukushii kokoro*). Here "beautiful" describes the supreme moral value that combines goodness, truth, and beauty. A Roman Catholic might call it being in a state of perfect ethical grace.

Some things considered in the West to be "good" and "true" are rejected by Japanese society in the name of beauty: an ethical "good" must be beautiful to be acceptable. Conversely, something "bad" that looks attractive may be lauded. Japanese mix aesthetic and ethical criteria; appearances count enormously. Many matters that are essentially "not good" and "not true" become socially acceptable because they are considered "beautiful." Some things without substance are camouflaged by elegant language. When packaged beautifully, gifts that have little value or utility, for example, are quite acceptable.

The Aesthetics of Process

In Japan the way something is done—actions, behavior, know-how—not just the result (or product), is much admired. I call this the aesthetics of process.

Process is frequently called form (*kata*, 型). In judo and Japanese-style fencing, kendo, the performer must master many stylized moves. The formal tea ceremony is another example. The tea is esteemed for its aroma and flavor, but the form of the ceremony—the way the tea is prepared—is an artistic experience. Guests observe the host's graceful movements in brewing and presenting the tea, see its beautiful color, smell the fragrance, taste the crisp flavor, and feel the clay of the cup in their hands.[2] Four of the five senses are engaged in this sophisticated pleasure.

The knife ceremony (*hōchō gishiki*), a set of movements in the preparation and cooking of food, has been formalized into an art to entertain guests. Shinto priests also perform

[2] Holding a tea cup in both hands enables the guest to feel its grainy surface. The handle on a Western tea cup permits a person to sip the beverage without burning one's fingers. Although this is a very practical design, no thought was given to the tactile pleasure given by the texture of the porcelain clay. The rough feel of the bottom of a tea cup, which is sometimes left unfinished, gives particular pleasure to aficionados.

the knife ceremony at New Year to amuse the gods honored in their shrine. The Japanese *teppanyaki* restaurant Benihana, where the meat is cooked on a steel plate in front of the customers, uses the chefs' chopping skills as a clever marketing technique at its branches in the United States. The chef cuts the meat—slicing thin pieces, trimming off fat—with a panache that amuses diners. A traditional skill is put to new uses. The chef's movements and flair make the production process a kind of game—a mixture of practicality and play—that both staff and audience enjoy. Similarly, the Japanese style of bathing has a dual purpose. Getting clean is the primary objective, but the bath (particularly the large communal bath at a hot-spring resort) is also a form of group relaxation.

Some kinds of physical labor, like the planting of rice seedlings or QC circle activities in a factory, seem to have been converted into an art form, a pleasant ritual that the participants enjoy. Westerners and Western economic theory regard work as toil, as just a means of producing goods. But the early Japanese put an element of play into their work, combining pleasure with productive activity to make even arduous, menial tasks bearable. This approach has been preserved through the centuries.

Japanese do not accept the Western notion that work is intrinsically abhorrent and working hours should be steadily reduced. U.S. and European complaints about workaholism in Japan are an attempt to impose a Western cultural value. Of course, Japanese do not think work is sheer fun, but they prefer not to view it as unrelieved drudgery either. In the Japanese ethos, elements of avocation and festival are mixed into a job or occupation. The gods themselves look upon work as their province. Work, play, utility, and art coexist, just as there is a symbiotic relationship between nature and artifice.

Intangible and abstract form (*kata*) has always been more

respected in Japan than the tangible and concrete. Christianity and Buddhism have inspired great works of art—painting, sculpture, and architecture—that are a legacy of faith. By contrast, Shintoism has no decorative art: virtually nothing from earlier times associated with Shintoism is extant. (Buddhist temples and monasteries have many national treasures; Shinto shrines have hardly any.) However, Shintoism has preserved intangible forms and traditions that date from antiquity. Christianity and Buddhism are proud of the age of some churches and temples. If one has to be rebuilt because the original has been destroyed by war or natural disaster, the new edifice is denigrated as "not the original" or "just a copy." And contemporary construction methods are used in the rebuilding. Shinto rejects such modernity. The oldest and most important Shinto building is the Inner Shrine at Ise, Mie Prefecture, which is believed to date from the third century and honors a mythical ancestor of the Imperial family. Made of cypress wood, it is rebuilt every twenty years exactly to the original specifications and by traditional ancient methods. The carpenters' work clothes are of ancient style, and they use the same kind of tools as in early times (very inefficient ones!). The shrine has been rebuilt by the same methods sixty times. What has been preserved at Ise over the centuries is not an ancient building, but the entire process of making it. A major characteristic of Japanese culture is the transmission to succeeding generations not of objects but of forms—the know-how—essential to production or appreciation.

Our ancestors' concern with form can be seen in household businesses of the feudal period. Frequently the owner of an enterprise bypassed his natural son and bequeathed the shop and trade name to a capable head clerk who was not a blood relative. The clerk in such a case would also be given the family's name. Many shops in Japan are proud of operating under the same name for ten or more generations, but most owe their continuity to this practice of adopting an heir. This selection of a successor who would continue the form, not the substance—the name not, the reality—never occurred in modern Korea or China.

In Korea, only a lineal son could inherit the business. This family-centered mentality was one reason why hereditary businesses did not develop. Large corporations in the United States grew faster than European companies because the concept of family ownership was abandoned there sooner than on the continent. In Japan, entrepreneurs did not rigidly adhere to consanguineous inheritance. Frequently, a capable male (*yōshi*) was adopted in order to perpetuate the family name, enabling the owner to pass on the business to an efficient successor. Primacy of the enterprise over family is one reason why only Japan, of the three Confucian neighbors, was able to modernize quickly. A mentality that finds immortality in form and name rather than substance and reality is more spiritual than materialist.

Many powerful hereditary monarchies, like the Ch'in Dynasty in China and the Bonapartes in France, quickly collapsed and disappeared. The Roman Catholic Church has survived partly because it is a religious body, but also because the rules (*kata*) of papal succession are clear and fixed. In this sense, hereditary businesses in Japan have a semi-religious dimension. As the Catholic faith must be defended and preserved by Rome, the hereditary enterprise should endure and prosper forever. The early Japanese probably believed that forms could better withstand the passage of time and human and natural disasters than things.

Miniaturization

South Korean writer O-Young Lee's book *Small Is Better*

was a bestseller in Japan. According to Lee, "one aspect of the Japanese mind is an imaginative power that seeks to make things smaller." He calls it a preference for miniaturization, or reductionism.

According to Lee, Japanese find beauty in small flowers with simple, quiet colors, like wisteria (*fuji*) and bush clover (*hagi*). When Americans improve a plant species, they try to make a larger and more colorful flower, whereas Japanese frequently attempt to create varieties that have a frail, feminine quality like weeping cherry trees (*Prunus pendula*) or willows. We are good at scaling down things like the flat, open fan (*uchiwa*) into a folding fan (*ōgi*, or *sensu*) that is compact and portable. In literature, the famous poem of the court poet Kakinomoto no Hitomaro (ca. 685–705) has long been a favorite:

Ashibiki no
Yamadori no o no
Shidari o no
Naganagashi yo wo
Hitori ka mo nen

The wild hill pheasants
Drag their feet and drag their tails,
Splendid though they be,
Through this long, long weary night
Like me, lying here alone.[3]

By using the genitive particle *no* repetitively at the ends of lines, the poet successively limited the subject and contracted the concept. The use of multiple possessives is "a vehicle for reducing in scale all manner of thoughts and forms," Lee says, and this is an aesthetic peculiar to Japan.

[3] Translation by Tom Galt, from *The Little Treasury of One Hundred People, One Poem Each*, compiled by Fujiwara no Sadaie (Princeton University Press, 1982).

I have two folding fans in front of me, one from South Korea and one Japanese, that show differences in the cultures. Consider the artwork. The Korean fan is illustrated with bold, masculine strokes; the Japanese drawing is done in refined, female strokes. The Korean fan is large, with twice the surface area of the Japanese one. The Japanese product looks like a toy, not a device for stirring the sticky August air. Now let's examine the bamboo strands. The Japanese bamboo work is far more precise: each piece is smooth to the touch and meshes perfectly. On the Korean fan, the bamboo pieces are of different lengths and diameters, causing uneven spacing, and the paper is pasted on somewhat erratically. If you rub your finger across its bamboo strips, you may get a splinter. (Nevertheless, it has an elegant charm!) If I were choosing a fan, the larger, practical Korean one would win in a breeze. If I were choosing a compact automobile or a consumer electronics item, however, I would consider Japanese products superior because of the attention to detail.

The ability to scale things down, make them portable, then miniaturize them and manufacture attractive, reliable products is a special quality of Japanese culture, a point Lee also makes. Not surprisingly, Japanese excel at industries like the manufacture of very large-scale integrated circuits (VSLI) In one sense, reductionism is a traditional process in Japan. This skill at making things smaller is seen in the box lunch (*bentō*), in which many kinds of food are carefully arranged in a small box. Japanese have a gift for enclosing a universe in a microcosm, according to Lee.

The people of Korea, too, are crowded into a limited land area, but the similarity with Japanese stops there. In thought and behavior, Koreans are expansive. They have a sense of beauty devoid of artifice, a feel for the majestic and grand. This shows in Korean pottery and literature, in the way Koreans entertain, and in their managerial style. There is a strong dislike of restrictive rules, in art and in everyday life. Japanese follow a certain prescribed sequence in eating a meal, for example. Koreans do not, their attitude being, "If food tastes delicious, the order in which I eat it makes no difference." In Noh and Kabuki, the actors' movements are governed by artistic conventions and the acting is highly stylized. But many Korean performing arts seem to stress improvisation. Classical Chinese poetry has strict rules for rhyming. Most of the Chinese poetry written by Japanese in centuries past carefully followed conventional style, whereas a great many Korean poets, who hated this kind of boring formalism, just ignored the rules. The same free spirit enfuses Korean cookbooks. A Japanese recipe gives everything in detail: "Add three-quarters of a teaspoon of salt." A Korean recipe gives the cook latitude: "Add an appropriate amount of salt." Even cookbooks reflect the Japanese penchant for conformity, standardization, and the artificial in contrast to Korean individualism, diversity, and naturalism. With a standard five-person set of tableware in Japan, each of the five utensils is exactly the same size. South Korean utensils are rarely precisely alike. A Korean would say, "Why does every piece have to be the same?" From a train window the countryside in the two lands looks very similar. But a careful observer notices that in Japan all the telephone poles are perfectly aligned and in South Korea some poles, like individuals who do not like queues, lean to one side or the other. I imagine South Koreans would say, "There's no reason for telephone poles to be in an absolutely straight line."

Korean individualism is a refreshing contrast to Japanese society's suffocating conformism, the pressure to follow norms and do what everybody else does. But differences in national character loom large when industrial precision is the objective. Japanese are extremely good, not only at making defect-free auto parts and microchips, but also at cooperating in small groups like QC circles or corporate task forces. According to Lee, Japanese always failed at large-scale projects. His advice is, "Don't become demons, become Issumbōshis! That is the way Japan's distinctive culture can make the greatest contribution to mankind." (The reference is to a famous Japanese folktale about a very tiny boy, Issumbōshi, a counterpart of Tom Thumb, who vanquished giant demons.)

Lee finds reductionism the idiosyncratic element of Japanese culture, but I would say it is a penchant for uniformity, the sense that everything should be in perfect alignment. Perhaps attention to detail in dinnerware sets and the position of telephone poles is worthwhile, yet it is the Japanese nature to want to align things when there is absolutely no need for uniformity. Although individuality is obviously preferable in the way white-collar employees dress or the way children are taught at the elementary school level, we want to standardize these, too. We do not feel comfortable with diversity. Look around any large office in a Japanese company. All the male employees will be wearing dark blue suits, almost as if there is a gentleman's agreement to patronize the same tailor. There is no personal taste or flair. Conformity is not imposed by the company: the culture compels it.

Craftsmanship

German cameras like Leica and Contax were world-famous long before Japanese makers challenged them. The outside casing of a German camera was beautifully finished, but parts of the interior were not; German rationalism dictated that a manufacturer economize where feasible. But Japanese cameras were beautifully finished on the inside too, even the places not visible to the user. All camera makers in Japan took this extra trouble. Why? Because Japanese customers would not have been satisfied with an "unfinished" product. For centuries Japanese tailors have used good cloth for and carefully stitched the inner lining of the half-coat (*haori*), which does not show. Even today the finer tailors take great care with the inner lining and stitching. Western tailors do an excellent job with design and fit—what can be seen—but they skimp elsewhere.

On visits to Japanese and U.S. warships as a child, I noticed that meticulous care was taken with the appearance of the interior fittings on Imperial Japanese Navy vessels, but on U.S. Navy ships they were merely functional. Japanese pipes are straight and valves were hidden; American pipes curved around obstacles and the valves were exposed. Of course, these were fighting ships, not luxury liners, so an interior decorator's approach to the plumbing is superfluous. Still, cultural differences appear even in the bowels of a warship.

Japanese take pains with the hidden places, and they like to make fixtures attractive. Partly this is because customers demand it, but it is also because the worker, be he a blue-collar factory hand or an artisan, enjoys finishing a task properly. Difficult as many readers may find this to accept, such pride in a job well done—call it craftsmanship or perfectionism—is a major force in organizational and business activity in Japan. The "sincerity" I described earlier (see Chapter 6) is also an attitude toward work—conscientiousness. On machinery made in Japan, even the cross line in screw heads is absolutely straight. It is not enough that parts be functionally flawless; they must also be aesthetically attractive. A playful and artistic consciousness results in craftsmanship. I am not talking about artisans in Kyoto a thousand years ago. Today's industrial workers have this same artistic sense. Beauty is its own justification. Although not necessary for practical reasons—to improve sales, for example—employees will do things that improve the product. Whether it is called groupism or "Japan, Inc.," this perfectionism has made Japan a manufacturing power.

Creating an Atmosphere

In Japanese companies and organizations, it is important to create an overall mood of aesthetic awareness, rather than individual incentives. This is next in importance after perfectionism.

In American society, individuals clash in a test of wills and personalities, which is resolved by negotiations. In Japanese society, the emphasis is on accommodation, on understanding the other party's position. Large numbers of people band together (individuality is not a factor), in a corporation, for example, and they help each other. By this process the economy as a whole develops. Although the two societies have much in common—approval of progress and development—these differences put them forever at odds over industrial policy. Japanese-style organizations carry out and expand their activities by creating a positive and creative atmosphere—as if the firm were holding a festival. Groups of co-workers throw themselves into the collective enterprise. Japanese society is not led by a powerful leader; it moves in response to this kind of general atmosphere.

According to an advertising agency's analysis of U.S. and Japanese TV commercials, American viewers would "be totally unable to understand what Japanese sponsors were trying to sell," because commercials in Japan stress mood and image rather than a direct hard sell. An advertising industry agreement prohibits comparison ads, i.e., messages that make a logical appeal to consumers based on data. Mood ads are short on substance: a series of beautiful, abstract words, set against a scene of natural beauty. Commercials aiming at the emotions are more effective than logical appeals at opening consumers' purses and wallets.

Japanese appreciate some things that they cannot explain rationally. It is like the feeling you have after reading a difficult, baffling book, that "it probably is a superb piece of work." The average Japanese today can follow very little of the sutras that Buddhist priests read at funerals. But the layman appreciates the texts more *because* he cannot understand them. A student from Sri Lanka once said he found it strange that Japanese Buddhists sit silently, in apparently thankful reverence, listening to sutras whose meaning they have not the foggiest idea of. By contrast, the sutras of Pali Buddhism or passages from the Bible are comprehensible to the careful listener.

A *waka* by the revered Buddhist priest Saigyō (1118–90) is a classical expression of the notion that what we cannot understand is therefore very valuable:

> Who lives here?
> In this sacred place I feel
> An awesome presence:
> I stand astonished
> At the joy of silent communion.

Japanese have an aversion to the over-lawyerly, vigorously analytical method of dealing with issues. Neither logic nor oratory developed in Japan. Rationality is frequently disparaged. Thus, we are often misunderstood by Westerners. The Portuguese Jesuit missionary Luis Frois (1532–97) came to Japan in 1563 and wrote extensively about the customs and events he observed. In his book *Contradicoes e Diferencas de Custumes Antre a Gente de Europa e Esta Provincia de Japao* (*Europe and Japan: A Cultural Comparison*), he says that it would be an insult for a European to tell a man to his face that he is a liar, but the Japanese treat the charge as social banter and laugh. According to Frois, while

Europeans try to speak precisely and avoid ambiguity, the Japanese prize vague expressions.

The Korean delegation that came to Japan when Tokugawa Yoshimune (1684–1751) was named shogun and Sin Yu-han, who visited Japan in the eighteenth century, both reported that deception and insincerity were ingrained Japanese customs and that the people were insouciant liars. Outsiders have often regarded Japanese as an untrustworthy people who use vague expressions and give evasive answers in order to dissemble. But to us, a direct "no" to a stranger or a visitor from another land who had made a long, dangerous journey, as in Frois's case, was considered discourteous. Japanese responses probably could have been interpreted as either "yes" or "no." If two mutually high-context Japanese were communicating, one would have immediately understood the other's implicit "no." But foreigners, of course, would not.

Luis Frois made other interesting observations. European clothing, he said, always has finer cloth on the outside than for linings, but in the apparel of Japanese dignitaries the lining is, if anything, better than the outer cloth. Europeans show their anger openly, but the Japanese, by unique methods, suppress their feelings, according to Frois. Europeans discipline their children by corporal punishment, a method rarely used in Japan, where rebukes are verbal. Observers today could make the same observations—so little effect does the passage of time have on culture.

Cherry blossoms are the most beloved flowers in Japan. Each spring co-workers, friends, and neighborhood groups get together for flower-viewing parties. Neither Chinese nor Koreans, despite a longstanding poetic affection for the plum blossom (which blooms in late winter), go in groups to view plum or cherry blossoms.

As the weather turns warm in early April and the cherry trees come to full bloom, millions of Japanese flock to public parks to relax under the blossoms. They party and drink saké (whiskey and beer, too) and sing loudly, the words often aided by portable amplifiers. Boisterous groups spill over into adjacent parties, and arguments break out among the drunken revelers. The scene of groups vying with others for mat space—trying to expand their party turf—is a miniature version of Japan's competitive industrial society. If people just want to watch cherry blossoms, they do not have to go to public parks jammed with thousands or tens of thousands of celebrants. A famous haiku says:

away from the crowd:
the cherry blossoms nod "hello"
as I stroll along

The writer points out that it is too noisy and crowded to enjoy the cherry blossoms on the front side of the mountain. On the deserted other side, the blossoms can be savored in quiet. In fact, however, few Japanese go to the tranquil spots; everybody prefers the raucous side of the mountain where they are jostled like rush-hour commuters.

A popular way of enjoying nature in Britain, in contrast, is bird-watching, which by its nature is a solitary activity. Bird-watching requires silence in order to both see and hear the birds.

Japanese are not primarily interested in the cherry trees. We like to get a group together and settle down in a spot amidst other groups. Cherry-blossom viewing is just an excuse for a communal outing.

This lively annual event combines the warm spring climate and group activity. To visit the quiet side of the mountain would be lonely and unpleasant, not spiritually uplifting. From childhood Japanese participate in this rite of spring with close friends and associates. We gather under the gently wafting cherry petals, sometimes in quiet conversation and other times in drunken revelry. Gradually group activity becomes part of the individual and collective consciousness.

Chapter Eight

Mutual Understanding Between Cultures and Corporations

I shall begin this chapter by describing an overall perspective on business transactions and management. Next, I shall apply that point of view to contemporary Japanese-style management. This discussion will show in what ways customary Japanese business practices are culturally incompatible with those of the United States, for example. It should also explain a major source of trade friction.

I shall also touch upon how nineteenth-century Japan, using indigenous management techniques, challenged and caught up with the West. This would have been impossible if Japan's nascent business world had tried to adopt foreign management methods. It was precisely the differences—groupism, skill at improving products—that gave Japan its chance. By striking at those windows of opportunity presented by Western culture, Japan was able to pull abreast of the developed nations. I shall also discuss the question of why Japan was able to modernize itself while neighboring China and Korea failed. This question has long fascinated scholars and business people.

We are not certain which aspects of humankind's behavior are hereditary and which are acquired. It is still unclear what factors are based on the social heritage of culture. Despite the advances in psychology, social psychology, sociology, and anthropology, a precise breakdown of innate and learned behavior remains elusive.

Many kinds of behavior are universal, transcending culture. The friendly smile is a common signal to another person that you bear him no ill will and will not attack. In nearly every society a person in a cramped space such as a crowded elevator will establish eye contact with others and nod slightly as a greeting. This gesture shows that he is not hostile. (Japanese are an exception: in an elevator, we usually maintain a blank expression because of shyness toward strangers.)

The bashfulness or sulkiness of infants is universal and unlearned behavior. A growing child has conflicting feelings toward others. On the one hand, there is a desire to draw close and rely on parents; on the other hand, the child wants to break the connection and be independent. Which desire dominates is determined by the cultural environment. Psychiatrist Doi Takeo calls the former inclination "the psychology of dependence," or *amae*. His well-known book *The Anatomy of Dependence* is based on clinical psychoanalytical data from several countries. According to Doi, although "Japanese society is permeated by the concept of *amae*," it is "a psychological phenomenon . . . basically common to mankind as a whole." Dependence is a universal emotion that predates culture, Doi says. I think the Western emphasis on individualism encourages adults to suppress it, but a groupist culture like Japan diffuses a dependent mentality. Common, hereditary factors that transcend culture largely determine human and organizational conduct.

To understand the various dimensions of human behavior, we must analyze its determinant components. First, there are innate, hereditary factors like basic emotional makeup. Second, there are social and cultural elements such as functional behavior. Third, there are the neurophysiological aspects that determine an individual's traits. Organizations can be similarly analyzed.

Cross-cultural interaction between organizations also requires comparative analysis to classify the factors present in both cultures (and the missing elements, too). In international business activities, the participating parties must find common ground and accept the unfamiliar. Although shared political and economic interests are important, they are not sufficient to make a joint venture work. Mutual understanding and respect are crucial and can often overcome political and economic disagreements.

First Encounters of an Awkward Kind

When two individuals or groups encounter each other for the first time, they simultaneously demonstrate power and friendly intent. National teams entering a stadium for the Olympics or other international athletic competition are led by a child or young woman who carries the country's name-placard. This is the perfect symbol of national pride and peaceful intentions.

In all cultures, at initial meetings people express both combative and peaceful inclinations. However, in a cross-cultural setting whether this is done awkwardly or with panache depends on people's experience in dealing with individuals of other cultures. Long isolated in Northeast Asia, Japanese are extraordinarily inept at first meetings. Accustomed to dealing only with each other, they try to handle business or diplomatic contacts as if they were meeting other Japanese. Instead of responding with a mixture of strength and openness, we concentrate on showing sincerity. This is self-indulgent behavior based on good intentions and the optimistic expectation that the other party will respond in kind. But to non-Japanese, this approach seems inexplicably casual or unfocused. It also arouses suspicions. Instead of getting down to brass tacks in a negotiation, the Japanese participants try to establish an atmosphere of good feelings as the foundation for future dealings, as they would if doing business with another Japanese individual or organization. Lacking a concrete strategy, they jump from one approach to another, in response to the other side's reaction. Foreigners often conclude that Japanese have no principles and will try anything that works. Consequently, many initial business negotiations somehow leave a bad taste. The Japanese think: "Despite our best efforts to show our sincerity, they didn't understand (i.e., respond sympathetically to our position) and just pushed their own demands." The foreign party thinks: "The Japanese say 'case by case' about everything. You can never pin them down to clear principles. They say one thing today and something else tomorrow. They always find a new excuse. We don't know what they're thinking."

At this introductory stage, much as in a tribal encounter, both parties recognize that the other will not kill them. Then they can move on to the next phase of communication and substantive action. The decision about what kinds of groups or organizations must be formed to effect this process is the responsibility of our politicians and business leaders.

A person's social and cultural activities as a member of a group can be classified into communication behavior and substantive behavior. Business activity and scientific research, for example, belong to the latter. Communication always precedes substantive behavior, and success in transcultural contacts requires particularly high-level communication skills.

Communication Via Language

A spoken language is the primary means of communication, and, as noted in Chapter 3, languages often form cultural zones. Language became a political issue in the modern period, when the nation-state became the unit of international politics. In order to standardize government administration and create a sense of national unity, each country decided on one common or official language. The designated tongue became both a symbol of national solidarity and a means of creating it. To modernize a country, the people who run the business, military, and educational systems need a common language. Before the rise of nationalism and the nation-state, linguistic differences were tolerated. People who spoke different languages lived peacefully together. There was little derision of or discrimination against groups solely because they spoke a minority language or dialect. But in the age of nation-states, each country has its national language. Language barriers must be surmounted and international communication improved in order to facilitate substantive contacts.

Communication can be verbal or nonverbal. The linguist J. V. Neustupný (the author of a volume in English on *Communicating with the Japanese* [Japan Times, 1987] and one in Japanese on *Communicating with Foreigners* [Iwanami, 1982]) notes that proficiency in the latter is often more important. Although Japanese are not good at verbal communication, they are skillful at nonverbal communication, Neustupný says. He points out that both verbal behavior and nonverbal behavior are different in the West and Japan. According to Neustupný, many Japanese attribute their communication failures to poor ability at foreign languages. But at the same time, he notes, some foreign languages and cultures present more problems for Japanese than others. The communication rules for Great Britain, including verbal and nonverbal forms, differ considerably from those for the European continent, and seem to be most difficult of all for Japanese to follow. The formulation explains why Japanese enjoy Anton Chekhov and Romain Rolland but have difficulty with Charles Dickens and Jane Austen.

Culture determines what people communicate. In the Japanese tradition, a refined person does not show joy or sorrow by facial expression. The Japanese practice of saying "no" with a slight smile is said to be often misunderstood by Westerners. If that is true, then a Thai refusal of a request must be truly bewildering: Thais say "absolutely no" and laugh heartily. This pattern may stem from an Oriental solicitude that tries to soften unpleasantness. Japanese and Americans nod their head to indicate "yes," but some Greeks shake their heads from side to side to show affirmation. Americans consider it polite to open a gift in front of the giver and show their pleasure by smiling and making appreciative remarks. Japanese never open a gift in the presence of the person who gave it. To do so would be extremely rude. There are many other examples of the wide diversity of communication rules.

Japanese have been taught to believe that "silence is golden" and to suppress the expression of feelings as much as possible. But participation in the world community has forced us to communicate accurately and convey our ideas to other people by clear speech and expressive body language. In the preferred communication mode among Japanese, the other party, by the logic of perception, correctly interprets emotions and intentions not shown or articulated verbally.

Logical speech is relatively unimportant when Japanese talk among themselves. Generally, Japanese converse because close associates enjoy talking together rather than as a dialogue to sort out differences. With strangers, Japanese are relatively poor at small talk intended to make a good impression, at stating opinions, or at arguing a position.[1]

At receptions or cocktail parties held as preludes to international conferences, Japanese tend to congregate together and avoid mingling with people they do not know. In addition to lacking confidence in our ability to express ourselves well in foreign languages, we are reluctant to initiate conversations with strangers.

Conversational language, whose main purpose has been for discussion among close friends or associates, avoids precise expression in favor of vague, indirect locution. Sugarcoated phraseology that will not irritate or offend is preferred. The Osaka dialect is particularly rich in words that can be interpreted in two ways (the better to avoid giving offense). Yet Osaka residents always know intuitively which meaning to take.[2]

Western languages have evolved into modes of expression suitable for disputation or confrontation. Westerners believe that progress is made, in business and other affairs, by argumentation, the vigorous exchange of opinions. The Japanese language was shaped for compromise and agreement. Japanese believe that people can accomplish their

[1] Japanese weekly and monthly magazines often carry roundtable discussions on current topics in which four or five persons talk about an issue. One might assume that the publications would assemble participants with sharply divergent views in hopes of sparking controversy. However, usually several people with similar views are brought together. The magazine hopes the participants will reach a firm consensus on the theme. Readers are thought to prefer a harmonious discussion that leads to a conclusion acceptable to everyone rather than heated arguments that expose deep differences and end with everyone agreeing to disagree.

[2] *Nakanaka* (considerably, very), for example, can mean something is "very bad" or "very good." For example, "There was a *nakanaka* number (many) of patrons, but the sales were *nakanaka* (bad)." The expression *kangaeteoku* (to consider) can mean "to weigh an idea carefully" or "not consider it." "I'll *kangaeteoku*" is often used when the speaker has no intention of doing something. *Ōkini* means both "Thank you" and "No, thank you." *Erai* means either "splendid, impressive" or "terrible, awful." The expression "That person is *erai*" can mean the person is either a sinner or a saint.

objectives by accepting each others' views and blending them into a workable agreement. Westerners and Japanese have fundamentally different expectations of language.

Japanese often find vagueness an advantage and clarity a hindrance. Japan has an army of 150,000, a navy whose equipment includes 14 submarines, and an air force with 270 combat aircraft. Nevertheless, the government's official position is that Japan has *self-defense forces* but not "land, sea, and air forces." This wording is used because the post-war Constitution, promulgated during the Allied Occupation, forbids Japan to have "land, sea, and air forces, as well as other war potential," and the Constitution has strong public support. But the use of vague terminology—"self-defense forces"—was a linguistic compromise that both proponents and opponents of rearmament could live with. Doves who fear a military establishment cite the *name* Japan Self-Defense Force as proof that the Constitution's pacifist spirit is intact; hawks who believe Japan must have military power point to the *reality*. Both sides, convinced their interpretation represents national policy, are partially satisfied.

A "Dangerous, Unpredictable People"

This compromise method is the key to doing business in Japan. Foreigners, understandably suspicious of Japanese ways, often regard us as a "dangerous, unpredictable people" because we normally do not express dissatisfaction or personal views, or even indicate such feelings with facial expression. Sometimes foreign managers have thought their Japanese employees were completely satisfied when actually the staff was stoically enduring terrible work conditions. When their patience was finally exhausted, the Japanese employees suddenly exploded in anger, to the consternation of foreign executives.

A shocking incident in February 1982 illustrates my point. A Japan Air Lines domestic flight was preparing to land at Haneda Airport when the captain suddenly reversed the engines, causing the aircraft to crash into Tokyo Bay, short of the runway. Twenty-four passengers were killed and 149 others injured. Investigation revealed that the pilot was schizophrenic, and his mental condition was a factor in the crash.

According to one U.S. airline executive, usually you can tell from the expression on an American pilot's face if he had an argument with his wife that morning; a pilot who is upset is grounded for the day. No sign of the JAL captain's mental condition was evident to his co-workers, however.

A copilot who notices that a captain is suddenly acting strangely should be able to stop him from endangering the plane and its passengers. But in work situations in Japan, the superior-subordinate relationship is binding: even if a superior behaves somewhat bizarrely, a loyal subordinate does not feel able to say or do anything about it. The JAL captain's rank kept his copilot from acting to avoid the crash until it was too late. Two pilots at the controls were unavailing in the JAL crash because only one had authority to act.

Two-seat jetliner cockpits were designed for American pilots. With Japanese crews, however, two pilots may have to be in separate cockpits so they can act independently. Cultural considerations are an important consideration in systems engineering.

Some machinery made for use in Japan proved to be very dangerous when exported to Africa. African workers were injured under circumstances where Japanese engineers and workers had operated the equipment without accident.

U.S. machinery and work systems have detailed manuals

or operating instructions, and workers follow the directions. In the past, detailed manuals were rarely prepared in Japan, but employees could still operate the equipment. Americans prefer instruction books and operating manuals that spell out exactly how something should be used. Japanese would rather tinker and puzzle out the procedures for themselves.

The difference can be seen in the way workers deal with rules. Many U.S. workers take work rules or instructions literally, often beyond the point of common sense. Japanese employees, on the other hand, observe the spirit of rules rather than the letter. From a management point of view, they should be given general guidelines, not a detailed blueprint. A broad outline works because Japanese society is high-context; not every detail has to be spelled out. The work force is also well educated, especially in the "three R's." Furthermore, Japanese workers are not primarily motivated by orders from superiors (or manual writers). They function autonomously and prefer to develop their own way of doing things—to write their own book. They dislike having to follow rules written by outsiders.

Contracts

The underlying assumption of written or explicit agreements—contracts are the best example—differs in Western societies and Japan. Mutual distrust is the premise in the West; mutual trust in Japan. In a hotel in the West, for example, guests lock their rooms; in Japanese inns there often are no room keys. Westerners assume they are at risk and take precautions; Japanese assume an honest environment and relax. This inclination to anticipate the worst pervades Western contracts, with their detailed provisions for every eventuality. The spirit is that of Murphy's law: whatever can go wrong will go wrong.

In Japan, a contract usually states overall objectives and general provisions. A guest at a traditional Japanese inn makes a blanket contract with the owners. There is a set fee per person for a night's stay. Whether the guest eats breakfast or skips it, orders tea and refreshments or not, the bill is the same. Japanese think that, in the long run, this arrangement benefits both sides. The traditional Japanese philosophy is that spelling out everything from A to Z in an agreement is a petty, pedantic exercise and presumes divergent interests. (However, in recent years Western attitudes about legal agreements have been spreading in Japan.)

An apartment lease in the United States runs to three or four pages and covers all the obligations of both sides. Americans think that unless every detail is agreed on in advance, there will be trouble later. Because disputes are so common, the United States has many times more lawyers per capita than Japan.

The standard apartment lease in Japan is a very simple document. Despite Westernization, Japan is a community-structured society: a lease need not be comprehensive. The parties can deal with any trouble that arises in a commonsense way on the basis of mutual trust. Sometimes, of course, positions are irreconcilable. In such a case usually a respected, neutral third party, known to both tenant and landlord, is asked to arbitrate. In the West, the parties directly involved draw up the contract; in case of disagreement, the matter is turned over to a lawyer. Contrasting styles of dispute resolution may be one reason why foreign corporations complain about the difficulty of doing business in Japan. From the Japanese point of view, however, the intrusion of foreign businessmen and lawyers, who want everything specified in written agreements, into a society that functions smoothly through verbal understandings and mutual trust is quite undesirable. This clash of assumptions about human nature is a non-tariff barrier.

To individualistic Westerners, all agreements—from business contracts to marriages—are exclusively between the signatories. In group-oriented Japan, a respected third party is added as a community representative. The *nakōdo*, a go-between or sponsor, plays this role at wedding receptions. Often the groom's work supervisor, by his presence and remarks the *nakōdo* gives a civil blessing to the ceremony. In the business world, a general trading firm (*sōgō shōsha*) frequently is the intermediary that arranges deals between two companies, a role which includes accepting limited financial responsibility. In the United States the usual pattern is for manufacturers to deal directly with retailers; in Japan there is invariably a wholesaler between the maker and the retail outlet. Many U.S. businessmen believe the formal involvement of wholesalers in every business transaction in Japan is a major impediment to the sale of American products.[3]

Whether a wholesaler plays an expanded role is largely a matter of commercial custom. In the United States lawyers commonly are the intermediary, but this is rare in Japan. Commercial practices are part of a country's historical development, and they may not be economically rational by contemporary standards. They vary by country and by region, and by industry within one country. Japan uses a respected third party as an intermdiary in transactions ranging from multimillion-dollar construction deals to nuptials because the arrangement is not regarded as

[3] Some Western trade officials and business executives ignore the cultural dimension and see everything in economic terms. This leads to wholesale condemnation of everything Japanese as a trade barrier: language, customs, housing styles, child rearing practices, public swimming pool regulations! Where is the respect for a trading partner's way of life? Cultural differences—language, lifestyles, food preferences—should not be confused with economic restrictions like tariffs, customs procedures, and product standards.

simply a private matter. It is also significant to the larger society. With a third party present to monitor this aspect, lawyers are not needed.

The pattern of transactions in the commodity exchanges of the West and Japan reflect societal norms. In Europe and the United States, individuals buy and sell commodities. In Japan, frequently commodities are bought and sold by groups of sellers and buyers; i.e., both sides are organized into large units. This difference also stems, I think, from the individualism of the West and the groupism of Japan. Because Japan's commercial customs are difficult for outsiders to understand, foreigners often charge that this country's markets are closed to their products. In one sense, calls for market liberalization are a demand that Japan change its group orientation and become more individualistic. Since that conversion is unlikely, trade friction will persist.

Individualism facilitated the development of capitalist, industrial societies in Europe and the United States. Japan caught up to the West by skillfully using communal patterns such as paternalism and worker loyalty. If Japan had adopted Western values, it could not have modernized so rapidly.

There is much interest in the process by which Japanese corporations (and other organizations) challenged the West's lead. Japanese modernizers first meticulously studied the way their Western counterparts operated, found the vulnerable points, and struck hard. An economist would say they looked for comparative advantages. What strategy will the next group of industrializing countries use?

Herman Kahn predicted that the next industrializers would be from the Confucian cultural sphere—South Korea, Hong Kong, and Singapore (see Chapter 4). These countries share common values—diligence, civility, frugality, and abstinence—which correspond to the Protestant ethic's emphasis on self-denial. South Korean economist Kim Il-gon, in his book *Order and Economy in the Confucian Cultural Sphere*, also discusses future industrialization of the Confucian bloc.

Japan's Rapid Modernization

Of the countries in the Confucian region, why did only Japan achieve rapid modernization? My answer is that Japan was *not* a fundamentally Confucian nation, and that that expedited our industrialization. Buddhism and Confucianism spread to Japan, but only the compatible features were adopted; Japanese were never totally converted to either. This is true of Christianity, Marxism, and other Western thought systems as well. Japan caught up with the West in a unique way. Now that there are no more models to emulate, we are searching for our own goals and style.

There are three major differences between the societies of China and Korea and that of Japan. First, the former have always been centralized, whereas in Japan, from ancient times to the present, power has been diffused. In the People's Republic of China and the two Koreas, power is concentrated in a dictatorial leader who rules by patriarchal authority in a centralized government, a pattern dating from the medieval period. These leaders manifest the Confucian ideal of the extraordinarily wise and virtuous ruler who has the mandate of Heaven to govern.

In Japan, samurai families came to power in the twelfth century, and administration was divided among many local daimyo under a single shogun. Daimyo were leaders who governed essentially autonomous fiefs. Power was decentralized throughout old Japan; distinctive local economies and cultures developed. This pattern contrasts with China and Korea, where a relatively small number of nobles and officials clustered around the ruler controlled the peasant population. Until about the fifteenth century, Japan and Korea were agrarian societies at the same economic level. From about the seventeenth century, Japan's commerce and industry developed rapidly and productivity increased, while Korea remained an agricultural country. In Japan, from the fifteenth century the economy of the daimyo-led fiefs expanded, transforming them into powerful feudalistic polities. As feudal lords, the daimyo sought to strengthen their economic base. They encouraged handicraft industry, protected merchants in the castle towns, reduced market taxes, and improved distribution of food and other goods. Japan's numerous wholesalers and complex distribution network can be traced to this historical process.

When the West expanded into Asia in the mid-nineteenth century, China and Korea were stagnant agricultural societies. However, Japan's handicraft industry and commercial infrastructure were already highly developed. When the Powers ended Japan's seclusion in the 1850s, the country was able to begin to industrialize with relative ease.

No merchant class developed in Yi-dynasty Korea. The centralized bureaucracy, ruled by a hereditary monarch and administered by officials selected by a Chinese-style literary examination system, was hostile to commercial enterprise. The distribution of agricultural products and other goods was strictly regulated; it was impossible for strong private wholesalers or even retailers to flourish. There was no business elite like the wealthy merchant houses of Edo (Tokyo) and Osaka during the Tokugawa period. Although controlled by and nominally deferential to the samurai class, these merchant communities were enormously powerful in their own right. Even today the status of a South Korean businessman is lower than that of his Japanese counterpart, and the prestige of intellectuals, successors to

Table 8. Distribution systems in Japan and South Korea

			Japan		South Korea	
			1968	1976	1968	1976
Total	Number of establishments	Wholesale trade (a)	234,982	338,169	13,193	20,260
		Retail trade (b)	1,432,436	1,614,067	264,100	393,651
	Ratio: (a) / (b)		(16%)	(21%)	(5.0%)	(5.1%)
			(unit: ¥ 1 billion)		(unit: ₩ 1 billion)	
	Total sales during the year	Wholesale trade (c)	62,816	222,315	184	2,449
		Retail trade (d)	165,107	560,329	243	3,310
	Ratio: (c) / (d)		(38%)	(40%)	(75%)	(74%)
Metropolitan areas (Tokyo and Seoul)	Number of establishments	Wholesale (e)	39,863	60,282	4,126	6,834
		Retail (f)	134,724	153,310	65,133	99,937
	Ratio: (e) / (a)		(17%)	(20%)	(31%)	(34%)
	Ratio: (f) / (b)		(9.4%)	(9.5%)	(25%)	(25%)
			(unit: ¥ 1 billion)		(unit: ₩ 1 billion)	
	Total sales during the year	Wholesale (g)	21,387	77,351	83	1,367
		Retail (h)	2,736	7,661	96	1,257
	Ratio: (g) / (c)		(34%)	(35%)	(45%)	(56%)
	Ratio: (h) / (d)		(16%)	(14%)	(40%)	(38%)

Sources: Japan and South Korea editions, *Census of Commerce*.
Currency exchange rates used: 1 US $ = 250 ¥ = 800₩.

The Tokyo metropolitan area has about 10 percent of Japan's total population. The Seoul metropolitan area has about 20 percent of South Korea's total population.

the *yangban* literati of the Yi dynasty, is much higher than that of intellectuals in Japan.

Table 8 compares the distribution systems of Japan and South Korea.

The ratio of wholesale trade to retail trade (calculated by number of establishments or by annual sales) is high in Japan and low in South Korea. Since the Tokugawa period, there have been a large number of traditional wholesalers with deep roots in the local economy. There is no comparable network in South Korea. Furthermore, a very high percentage of total business is concentrated in the Seoul metropolitan area. South Korea remains a highly centralized state, much as it was during the Yi dynasty. Although a central government in Japan has made national policy since the Meiji period (1868–1912), the concentration of commercial activity in Tokyo is not comparable to that in Seoul.

Power is also diffused within Japanese organizations, public or private. Generally speaking, top officials or executives have relatively little power over subordinates or local authorities, compared to similar organizations in China and Korea. Small work-site groups, not orders from the board room, sustain quality control in Japanese companies, for example. The typical corporation has a superstructure of centralized top managers, which skillfully uses the voluntary activity at factories and work sites.

Practical Ethics

A second major difference between Japan and China/Korea is in business ethics. Chinese ethics were shaped by Confucianism, of course, which was also the official ideology of the Yi dynasty and which permeated Korean values. Although the Tokugawa shogunate designated Confucianism as the orthodox teaching, its role was very different in Korea and Japan. The Korean temperament preferred the Zhu

Xi school of neo-Confucianism. Scholarly factions stressed the interpretation of the "Four Books" of the Confucian tradition and strict, formal ethics. In Japan, the Yang-ming school of Confucianism, named after the Ming neo-Confucianist thinker Wang Yang-ming, was dominant. Wang emphasized practical ethics, a reaction against "the unpractical and academic emphasis of the Zhu Xi system." This choice reflected the practical nature of Japanese.

A primary virtue in Confucian ethics is filial piety. When a Korean father died, according to strict Confucian tenets, the eldest son was expected to observe a long period of mourning near his parent's grave. He wore plain garments, ate only simple food, and did not bathe. Filial respect was expressed formalistically. But the Japanese, with their utilitarian outlook, twisted Confucian piety into a prescription for worldly success (Japanese flexibility). A merchant, for example, requited his obligations to his father's soul by becoming rich He accomplished this through trustworthiness, frugality, perseverance, and hard work. Ishida Baigan (1685–1744) was the leading proponent of this doctrine.

In the official Tokugawa status system, the four classes were samurai, peasants, handicraft workers, and merchants. Although the merchant class was formally at the bottom of the status order and punctiliously deferred to the samurai, many merchants, because of their wealth, were actually more powerful than daimyo. They also had formal standards of behavior—codified as house rules and equivalent to *bushido*—and a strong sense of self-esteem. In Yi-dynasty Korea, both the nominal place of merchants in the social order, according to Confucian teaching, and their actual status were low. Merchants were held in contempt by ordinary farmers. This Korean tendency to disdain practical affairs amounted to a rejection of the modern business mentality which assiduously pursues rational economic interests. This is a cultural reason why even today many South Korean merchants try to amass quick fortunes from speculation, especially in land, rather than make reasonable profits from honest, steady effort. This mentality can be expected to change somewhat as the South Korean economy matures.

Japan modernized and industrialized rapidly because it is a practical society. College graduates in the practical disciplines of law, economics, and engineering are respected. Both China and Korea were aesthetic societies, biased toward the elegant but impractical. Many important positions were held by men trained in literature. The Chinese traditional examination system, the path to officialdom, required an ability to write elegant prose and poetry, not knowledge of the law. This system produced the intellectual elite that governed China and Korea. Although they were rigorously schooled in Confucianism, knew the Chinese classics, and were excellent writers, this elite lacked the analytical training, which comes from the study of law, necessary to organize society—government bureaus, companies—and an understanding of modern technology. The ruling class in Japan were samurai concerned with martial and administrative affairs. From the first contacts with the West in the sixteenth century, the samurai were enormously interested in Western science and particularly in technology.

The *Ie* Company

A third major distinction between Japan and China/Korea is the emergence of the *ie*-type company. In my travels around South Korea I have been struck by the absence of old, established businesses. There are virtually no craft shops or restaurants that date their founding to the nineteenth century or earlier. In Japan and the West, countless stores and restaurants have operated under the same trade name for several centuries. The dearth of such establishments in South Korea reflects a premodern business outlook.

The family unit of blood relatives was important in Japan, China, and Korea from antiquity, but extended kinship organizations varied significantly. The Korean *munjung* system followed patrilineal succession, according to the orthodox intepretation of Confucianism. Strict observance of exogamy also differed from Japan's endogamous family system. In Japan, succession to a family name and emblem by a male with no blood ties was recognized from the eighth century. Because of this nominal lineage succession, the *ie*'s name became a trademark, business know-how was passed on, and some establishments survived for many generations. The Japanese way transmitted reputation and knowledge to the next generation. Blood-line succession in Korea meant that a business belonged to an individual; its reputation and methods were not passed to the merchant's son and grandson. Japanese considered preserving a family's business more important than a pure pedigree—additional proof that Japanese are born merchants!

Early twentieth-century Japanese and Korean shop signs show the commercial heritage of these ways of thinking. On the Japanese signs the store's name (the hereditary trade name) is always in large letters, with the proprietor's name in small characters. The Korean signs have the proprietor's name in large letters and no store name.

These differences explain, I believe, why of the Confucian countries only Japan was able to rapidly create a capitalist economy.

Congenial Cultures

Finally, I wish to comment on congeniality among cultures. Just as two individuals may get along well and feel the same way about things, there is a bonding between some cultures. We see this cultural affinity between the British and Indians, the French and Iranians, and the Germans and Turks. The reasons differ in each case. The British and Indians perhaps share a sense of grandeur, the former in their empire and the latter in their civilization. I was astounded by the Victoria Memorial in Calcutta. It was hard to believe that the Indians, who were rapaciously exploited and oppressed for so long by Great Britain, still had such respect for their erstwhile rulers. With the French and Iranians, the bond may be enormous pride in their cultures, or perhaps their individualistic natures. The Germans and Turks were allies in World War I, and perhaps they get along well because both have masculine cultures.

Textbook examples of incompatible national temperaments the those of Japanese and Koreans and those of Chinese and Russians. Many neighboring countries do not get along; examples are Germany and France and the United States and Mexico. Envy of a neighbor's success and affluence may partly explain the hostility. Nevertheless, adjoining countries must try to maintain a balanced open relationship, poisoned by neither arrogance nor resentment.

Intercultural exchange is a catalyst as old as mankind. The flow of ideas and products, carried by itinerant holy men or intrepid merchants, has destroyed societies and inspired new civilizations. Management textbooks always discuss the cultural dimension of international business. A corporation starting to operate in a foreign country faces practical problems. Should it conform to the local culture and mores or try to do things differently? The former approach follows the rule of "When in Rome, do as the Romans do." But the latter way is also valid. The Carthaginians believed that no matter how they tried to emulate local customs, they could not match the Romans. Instead, they assiduously promoted the best features of their own civilization. This is the innovative approach advocated by Professor

John Fayerweather and many other American specialists on international management. Merchants have always been secret agents of cultural destruction and creativity.

To avoid contact with other societies for fear of misunderstanding and conflict simply delays the acculturation process. Far better to welcome contacts and get quickly through the awkward stage. Intercultural understanding, so essential in a rapidly shrinking world, should be preached with messianic zeal.

All organizations—business, military, scientific, labor, or religious—have a unique organizational culture that is derived from the larger society. I may seem to have been arguing that a kind of cultural determinism governs corporate activities. I only want to stress that point because everyone, individuals and organizations, must objectively understand the predetermined elements of their own existence. Accurate self-awareness is the first step to creating a new destiny. When a corporation fully recognizes its karma—cultural heritage—then management can transcend the past and lead it to the promised land of responsible, profitable international operations.

Appendix

The JKC Businessmen Survey was conducted in 1979–81. As the chief researcher, I oversaw selection of the sample and preparation of questionnaires in three languages—Japanese, Korean, and Chinese. Only a small portion of the data has been presented in this book. In the hope that other scholars will make use of our findings in future research, I will outline our methodology.

The survey respondents were employees of Japanese, South Korean, and Taiwanese companies in six industrial categories: light industry (consumer products), heavy industry (machinery), trading companies, finance and insurance, wholesalers, and large retailers. (The last two categories were not included in the South Korean portion.) We selected five major companies in each category, and polled 30 white-collar employees in each company. The respondents were chosen by stratified random sampling; we attempted to obtain 10 persons in their twenties, 10 in their thirties, and 10 in their forties. The total sample included 900 respondents from each country.

The questionnaires contained approximately 150 questions in four subject categories: 1) marketing and business transactions and contracts, 2) company organization and decision-making, 3) international management, and 4) personal data for classifying the respondents. Nearly all questions were of the "yes/no" type.

Two major methodological difficulties emerged in this cross-national survey. The first was in standardizing terminology. For example, the Japanese term *shiteki* (私的) has a negative connotation, whereas the English equivalent, "private," has a positive meaning. The second, and much greater, difficulty was whether a question struck the same chord in respondents. For example, a question like the following is often asked in surveys: "Do you find your raison d'etre in work, or in activities unrelated to your job?" Generally, respondents in industrialized countries answer candidly, but respondents in developing countries usually repeat the ideal social norm—i.e., give the reply society expects.

The research team consisted of (in addition to myself) Professor Kojima Sotohiro, Dōshisha University; Professor Kim Won-sue, Seoul National University; Professor Shin Yu-kuwon, Seoul National University; Professor Kuo Kung-mo, National Chunghsing University; and Professor Liu Shuei-shen, National Chengchi University.

Although the complete survey results have not been published, the full data are available at the Yoshida Hideo Foundation in Tokyo. I published a summary in Japanese in the journal *Ryūtsū Seisaku* (Distribution Planning), Nos. 7–8, 1981.

Bibliography

Chapter One

Bendasan, Izaya [Isaiah Ben-Dasan] (Yamamoto Shichihei). *Nihonjin to Yudayajin* [The Japanese and the Jews]. Tokyo: Yamamoto Shoten, 1970. English translation, by Richard Gage, published by John Weatherhill, Inc. (Tokyo), 1972.

——— *Nihonkyō ni tsuite* [On Japanism]. Tokyo: Bungei Shunjūsha, 1975.

Bierce, Ambrose G. *The Devil's Dictionary*. First published 1911; reprinted by Dover Publications (New York), 1970.

Eliade, Mircea. *Le Mythe de l'Eternel Retour* [Myth of the Eternal Return]. Paris: Gallimard, 1949. English translation, by Willard Trask, published by Princeton University Press (Princeton), 1954.

Geertz, Clifford. *Interpretation of Cultures*. New York: Basic Books, 1973.

Hall, Edward T. *The Dance of Life: The Other Dimension of Time*. New York: Anchor Press/Doubleday, 1983.

Sources are listed under the chapter in which they are first mentioned.

Hirano Jinkei. *Zoku-Kodai Nihonjin no Seishin Kōzō* [Nature, Poetry, and Time in Antiquity]. Tokyo: Miraisha, 1976.
Hori Ichirō. *Nihon no Shāmanizumu* [Japanese Shamanism]. Tokyo: Kodansha, 1971.
Ishida Ichirō. *Kami to Nihon Bunka* [Gods and Japanese Culture]. Tokyo: Perikansha, 1983.
Iwata Keiji. *Kami no Jinruigaku* [Gods and Anthropology]. Tokyo: Kodansha, 1979.
———. *Kami to Kami* [Gods and God]. Tokyo: Kodansha, 1984.
Katō Kyūso, ed. *Nihon no Shāmanizumu to sono Shūhen* [Shamanism in Japan and Asia: A Comparative Study]. Tokyo: Nihon Hōsō Shuppan Kyōkai, 1984.
Keene, Donald. *Hyakudai no Kakaku: Nikki ni Miru Nihonjin* [Japanese Diaries]. 2 vols. Tokyo: Asahi Shimbun-sha, 1984.
Moore, W. E. *Man, Time and Society*. New York: Wiley, 1963.
Nakamura Hajime. *Hikaku Shisō-ron* [A Comparative History of Thought]. Tokyo: Iwanami Shoten, 1960.
Nakano Hajime. *Jikan to Ningen* [Time and Man]. Tokyo: Kodansha, 1976.
Tanabe Hajime. *Rekishiteki Genjitsu* [Historical Reality]. Tokyo: Iwanami Shoten, 1940.
Tanaka Gen. *Kodai Nihonjin no Jikan Ishiki* [Japanese Time Consciousness in Antiquity]. Tokyo: Kōbunkan, 1975.
Yamaori Tetsuo. *Nihon Shūkyō Bunka no Kōzō to Sokei* [Archetypes in Japanese Religion]. Tokyo: University of Tokyo Press, 1980.
———. *Kami to Hotoke* [Gods and the Buddha]. Tokyo: Kodansha, 1983.
Zerubavel, Eviatar. *Hidden Rhythms: Schedules and Calendars in Social Life*. Chicago: University of Chicago Press, 1981.

Chapter Two

Benedict, Ruth. *The Chrysanthemum and the Sword: Patterns of Japanese Culture*. Boston: Houghton Mifflin & Co., 1946.
Bonner, John T. *The Evolution of Culture in Animals*. Princeton: Princeton University Press, 1980.

Brislin, Richard W., and Paul B. Pedersen, *Cross-Cultural Orientation Programs*. Melbourne, Fla.: Robert E. Krieger, 1976.

Dubos, René. *Man Adapting*. New Haven: Yale University Press, 1980.

Hoopes, David S., Paul B. Pedersen, and George W. Renwick. *Overview of Intercultural Education, Training and Research* (3 vols.). Society for Intercultural Education, Training and Research, 1978.

Kang Chae-ŏn. *Chōsen no Kaika Shisō* [The Korean Enlightenment]. Tokyo: Iwanami Shoten, 1980.

Mizuno Shōichi et al. *Bunka to Keizai Hatten* [Culture and Economic Development]. Nagoya: University of Nagoya Press, 1983.

Nakamura Hajime. *Shūkyō to Shakai Rinri* [Religion and Social Ethics]. Tokyo: Iwanami Shoten, 1959.

Nakamura Yukihiko, ed. *Kinsei Chōnin Shisō* [Urban Thought in the Tokugawa Era]. Tokyo: Iwanami Shoten, 1975.

Noer, D. M. *Multinational People Management: A Guide to Organizations and Employees*. Washington, D.C.: Bureau of National Affairs, 1975.

Ōki Masao. *Nihonjin no Hōkannen* [The Concept of Law in Japan]. Tokyo: University of Tokyo Press, 1983.

Packard, Vance. *The Hidden Persuaders*. New York: David McKay, 1960.

Rhinesmith, S. H. *Cultural Organizational Analysis*. Cambridge, Mass.: McBer & Co., 1971.

Ruhly, S. *Orientations to Intercultural Communication*. Scientific Research Association, 1976.

Shibata Minoru. *Sekimon Shingaku* [The Philosophy of Ishida Baigan]. Tokyo: Iwanami Shoten, 1971.

Tylor, E. B. *Primitive Culture* (2 vols.), New York: Gordon Press, 1971.

Umehara Takeshi. *Nihon Bunka-ron* [Japanese Culture]. Tokyo: Kodansha, 1976.

Webber, R. A. *Culture and Management*. Homewood, Ill.: Richard D. Irwin, 1969.

Weber, Max. *The Protestant Ethic and the Spirit of Capitalism*. First published in German in 1904–5: most recent English publication, New York: Charles Scribner's Sons, 1977.

Weinshall, T. D. (ed.). *Culture and Management: Selected Readings*. Harmondsworth: Penguin Books, 1971.

Chapter Three

Condon, John C. *Cultural Dimensions of Communication*. Published in Japanese as *Ibunkakan no Komyunikeishon* [Communication between Cultures] by Simul Press (Tokyo), 1980.

Condon, John C., and Fathi S. *An Introduction to Intercultural Communication*. New York: Bobbs-Merrill Co., 1975.

Harris, Philip R., and Robert T. Moran. *Managing Cultural Differences*. Houston: Gulf Publishing Co., 1979.

Hayashi Kichirō. *Ibunka Intāfeisu Kanri* [Managing Cultural Exchange]. Tokyo: Yūhikaku, 1985.

Iizuka Kōji. *Yōroppa tai Hi-Yōroppa* [European Culture]. Tokyo: Iwanami Shoten, 1971.

Inemura Hiroshi. *Nihonjin no Kaigai Futekiō* [Japanese Culture Shock]. Tokyo: Nihon Hōsō Shuppankai, 1980.

Ishida Ei'ichirō. *Tōzaishō* [Essays on East and West]. Tokyo: Chikuma Shobo, 1967.

———. *Nihon Bunka-ron* [Japanese Culture]. Tokyo: Chikuma Shobo, 1969. English translation, by Teruko Kachi, published by University of Tokyo Press (Tokyo), 1974.

Jansen, Marius B. *Japan and Its World: Two Centuries of Change*. Princeton: Princeton University Press, 1980.

Miyazaki Ichisada. *Tōfū Seiga* [Essays on Here and There]. Tokyo: Iwanami Shoten, 1978.

Moritani Masanori. *Nichi-Bei-Ō Gijutsu Kaihatsu Kyōsō* [Technological Competition among Japan, the United States, and Europe]. Tokyo: Toyo Keizai Shimposha, 1981.

Nakata Mitsuo. *Bunka no Kyōō—Hikaku Bunka Gairon* [Cultures in Collision: An Interdisciplinary Approach to Comparative Culture]. Tokyo: University of Tokyo Press, 1982.

Nakao Sasuke. *Gendai Bunmei—Futatsu no Genryū* [Mainstreams of Modern Civilization]. Tokyo: Asahi Shimbunsha, 1978.

Okakura Kakuzō. *The Ideal of the East, with Special Reference to the Art of Japan*. London: John Murray, 1904; reprint ed., Tokyo: Charles E. Tuttle, 1970.

———. *The Book of Tea*. Fox Duffield & Co., 1906; reprint ed., New York: Dover, 1979.

Sakamoto Yasumi et al. *Kaigai Shinshutsu Kigyō no Jittai* [Managing Offshore: Guidelines for Success]. Tokyo: Toyo Keizai Shimposha, 1978.

Sakuma Ken. *Nihonteki Keiei no Kokusaisei* [Adapting Japanese Management to a Global Economy]. Tokyo: Yūhikaku, 1983.

Shiraishi Daiji. *Nihongo no Hassō* [The Spread of the Japanese Language]. Tokyo: Tokyodō Shuppan, 1961.

Sitaram, K. S., and R. T. Cogdoll. *Foundations of International Communication*. Columbus, Ohio: Charles E. Merrill Pub. Co., 1976.

Suzuki Takao. *Tosareta Gengo—Nihongo no Sekai* [Language Locked Up]. Tokyo: Shinchōsha, 1975.

Suzuki, Daisetz T. *Zen Buddhism and Its Influence on Japanese Culture*. Kyoto: The Eastern Buddhist Society, 1938.

Terpstra, Vern. *The Cultural Environment of International Business*. Cincinnati: South-Western Publishing Co., 1978.

Chapters Four, Five, and Six

Abegglen, James C. *The Japanese Factory: Aspects of Its Social Organization*. Glencoe, Ill.: The Free Press, 1958.

Aida Yūji. *Nihonjin no Ishiki Kōzō* [The Attitudinal Framework of the Japanese People]. Tokyo: Kodansha, 1970.

Amino Yoshiko et al. *Chūsei no Tsumi to Batsu* [Crime and Punishment in Medieval Japan]. Tokyo: University of Tokyo Press, 1983.

Bellah, Robert N. *Tokugawa Religion: The Values of Pre-Industrial Japan*. Glencoe, Ill.: The Free Press, 1957.

Clark, Rodney. *The Japanese Company*. New Haven: Yale University Press, 1979.

Doi Takeo. *Omote to Ura* [The Anatomy of Self: The Individual Versus Society]. Kyoto: Kōbundō, 1985.

Dore, Ronald. *Education in Tokugawa Japan*. London: Routledge and Kegan Paul, 1965.

———. *British Factory—Japanese Factory: The Origins of National Diversity in Industrial Relations*. Berkeley: University of California Press, 1973.

Hall, Edward T. *The Hidden Dimension.* New York: Doubleday & Co., 1966.

Hazama Hiroshi. *Nihonteki Keiei* [Japanese Management]. Tokyo: Nihon Keizai Shimbunsha, 1971.

Hirschmeier, Johannes, and Tsunehiko Yui. *The Development of Japanese Business, 1600–1973.* London: George Allen & Unwin; Cambridge: Harvard University Press, 1975.

Itami Hiroyuki. *Nihonteki Keiei o Koete—Kigyō Keieiryoku no Nichi-Bei Hikaku* [Beyond Japanese Management: A Comparison of Japanese and American Practices]. Tokyo: Toyo Keizai Shimposha, 1982.

Iwata Ryūshi. *Nihonteki Keiei no Hensei Genri* [Principles of Japanese Management]. Tokyo: Bunshindō, 1977.

Kagono Tadao et al. *Nichi-Bei Kigyō no Keiei Hikaku, Senryakuteki Kankyō Tekiō no Genri* [A Comparison of Japanese and American Management Methods]. Tokyo: Nihon Keizai Shimbunsha, 1983.

Kamei Katsuichirō. *Nihonjin no Seishinshi* [Spiritual History of the Japanese]. 6 vols. Tokyo: Bungei Shunjūsha, 1967.

Kamishima Jirō. *Bunmei no Kōgengaku* [Searching for Japan's Roots]. Tokyo: University of Tokyo Press, 1971.

————, ed. *Nihon Kindaika no Tokushitsu* [Japan's Modernization]. Tokyo: Institute of Developing Economies, 1973.

Kobayashi Shigenobu. *Nihonjin no Kokoro to Iro* [Color and Japanese Aesthetics]. Tokyo: Kodansha, 1974.

Koike Kazuo. *Nihon no Jukuren* [Training for Excellence]. Tokyo: Yūhikaku, 1981.

Maruyama Masao. *Nihon no Shisō* [Japanese Thought]. Tokyo: Iwanami Shoten, 1961.

Minami Hiroshi. *Nihonteki Jiga* [The Japanese Ego]. Tokyo: Iwanami Shoten, 1983.

Minamoto Ryoen. *Giri to Ninjō—Nihonteki Shinjō no—Kōsatsu* [Japanese Values: Moral Obligations Versus Human Feeling]. Tokyo: Chūō Kōronsha, 1969.

Mito Tadashi. *Nihonjin to Kaisha* [Corporations and Individuals]. Tokyo: Chūō Kōronsha, 1981.

Moles, A. A., and E. Rohmer. *Psychologie de l'espace.* Paris: Casterman, 1978.

Morishima Michio. *Nihon to Igirisu* [Japan and Britain]. Vols. 1 and 2. Tokyo: Iwanami Shoten, 1977, 1978.

Murakami Yasusuke et al. *Bunmei to shite no Ie Shakai* [*Ie* Society as a Pattern of Civilization]. Tokyo: Chūō Kōronsha, 1979.

Nakamura Hajime. *Tōyōjin no Shii Hōhō* [Ways of Thinking of Eastern Peoples]. 3 vols. Tokyo: Shunjūsha, 1962.

Nakane Chie. *Tate Shakai no Ningen Kankei* [Japanese Society]. Tokyo: Kodansha, 1967. English-language version published by University of California Press (Berkeley), 1970.

———. *Tate Shakai no Rikigaku* [The Dynamics of a Vertical Society]. Tokyo: Kodansha, 1978.

Ōtsuka Hisao et al. *'Amae' to Shakai Kagaku* ['Dependency' and Social Science]. Kyoto: Kōbundō, 1976.

Pascale, Richard T., and Anthony G. Athos. *The Art of Japanese Management*. New York: Simon & Schuster, 1981.

Sagara Tōru. *Seijitsu to Nihonjin* [Sincerity]. Tokyo: Perikansha, 1980.

Tajima Sadao, ed. *Jikan-Kūkan* [Time and Space]. Kyoto: Kōbundō, 1977.

Tsunoda Tadanobu. *Nihonjin no Nō* [The Japanese Brain]. Tokyo: Taishūkan Shoten, 1978. English-language version, translated by Yoshinori Oiwa, issued by the same publisher, 1985.

Tsurumi Kazuko. *Kōkishin to Nihonjin* [The Inquisitive Japanese]. Tokyo: Kodansha, 1972.

Urabe Kuniyoshi. *Nihonteki Keiei o Kangaeru* [On Japanese Management]. Tokyo: Chūō Kōronsha, 1978.

Ueyama Shumpei and Watabe Tadayo. *Inasaku Bunka* [Rice and Culture]. Tokyo: Chūō Kōronsha, 1984.

Watsuji Tetsuro. *Fūdo* [Ethos and Environment]. Tokyo: Iwanami Shoten, 1935.

Yoshino, Michael Y. *Japan's Managerial System: Tradition and Innovation*. Cambridge: MIT Press, 1968.

Chapter Seven

Frois, Louis. *Contradições e diferenças custumes antre a gente de Europa e esta provincia de Japão*. First published 1585; reprinted in 1955 by Sophia University, Tokyo.

Iida Ken'ichi. *Fūdo to Gijutsu to Bunka* [Environment, Technology and Culture]. Tokyo: Soshietesha, 1984.

Karaki Junzō. *Nihonjin no Kokoro no Rekishi* [A History of Japanese Thought]. 2 vols. Tokyo: Chikuma Shobō, 1976.

Kokusai Bunka Kenkyūjō (International Culture Institute), ed. *Shizen to wa Nanika* [The Meaning of Nature]. Kyoto: Hōzokan, 1985.

Lee, O-Young. *'Chijimi' Shikō no Nihonjin* [Small Is Better: Japan's Mastery of the Miniature]. Tokyo: Gakuseisha, 1982. English-language version published by Kodansha International (Tokyo), 1983.

Moritani Masanori. *Nihon·Chūgoku·Kankoku Sangyō Gijutsu Hikaku* [Industrial Technology in Japan, China, South Korea]. Tokyo: Tōyō Keizai Shimpōsha, 1980.

Nihon Bunka Kaigi (Japan Culture Congress), ed. *Nihonbi wa Kanō Ka* [The Possibility of a Japanese Aesthetic]. Tokyo: Kenkyūsha, 1973.

———. *Shizen no Shisō* [The Philosophy of Nature]. Tokyo: Kenkyūsha, 1974.

Pak U-hi and Moritani Masanori. *Gijutsu Kyūshū no Keizaigaku—Nihon·Kankoku Keiken Hikaku* [Absorbing Technology: The Experience of Japan and South Korea]. Tokyo: Tōyō Keizai Shimpōsha, 1982.

Sagara Tōru. *Nihonjin no Kokoro* [JapàneseOValues]. Tokyo: University of Tokyo Press, 1984.

——— et al., eds. *Shizen* [Nature]. Tokyo: University of Tokyo Press, 1983.

——— et al., eds. *Bi* [Beauty]. Tokyo: University of Tokyo Press, 1984.

Simon, Herbert A. *The Sciences of the Artificial.* Cambridge, Mass.: MIT Press, 1969.

Shiga Shigetaka. *Nihon Fūkei-ron.* [Japanese Aesthetics] Tokyo: Gakuseisha, 1894. Reprinted by Kodansha (Tokyo), 1976.

Sin Yu-han. *Kaiyūroku—Chōsen Tsūshinshi no Nihon Kikō* [An Account of a Korean Delegation to Japan]. Published 1719; reprinted by Heibonsha (Tokyo), 1974.

Tajima Sadao, ed. *Shizen to Hanshizen* [The Natural and the Antinatural]. Kyoto: Kōbundō, 1977.

Taut, Bruno. *Nihonbi no Saihatsugen* [Another Look at Japanese Aesthetics]. Tokyo: Iwanami Shoten, 1939.

———. *Nihon—Taut no Nikki* [Taut's Diary of Japan]. Tokyo: Iwanami Shoten, 1950–54.

Watsuji Tetsurō. *Nihon Rinri Shisōshi* [A History of Japanese Ethics]. 2 vols. Tokyo: Iwanami Shoten, 1952.

Chapter Eight

Birdwhistell, Ray L. *Kinesics and Context: Essays on Body Motion Communication.* Philadelphia: University of Pennsylvania Press, 1970.

Bloomfield, Leonard. *Language.* New York: Henry Holt & Co., 1933.

Brown, Ina C. *Understanding Other Cultures.* Englewood Cliffs, N. J.: Prentice-Hall, 1963.

Doi Takeo. *Amae no Kōzō* [The Structure of Dependence]. Kyoto: Kōbundō, 1976.

Fayerweather, John. *International Business Management.* New York: McGraw-Hill, 1969.

Frieg, J. P., and J. G. Blair. *There Is a Difference: Twelve International Perspectives.* Meridian House, 1975.

Hall, Edward T. *The Silent Language.* New York: Doubleday, 1959.

———. *Beyond Culture.* New York: Anchor Press/Doubleday, 1976.

Itō Kanji and Kurita Yasuyuki, eds. *Nihonjin no Zōtō* [Japanese Gift-giving]. Tokyo: Minerva Shobō, 1984.

Kim Il-gon. *Jukyō Bunkaken no Chitsujo to Keizai* [Order and Economy in the Cunfucian Cultural Sphere]. Nagoya: Nagoya University Press, 1984.

Leach, Edmund R. *Culture and Communication.* Cambridge: Cambridge University Press, 1976.

Nagasaka Satoru [Okazaki Hisahiko]. *Tonari no Kuni de Kangaeta Koto* [Distant Neighbors: Korea and Japan]. Tokyo: Nihon Keizai Shimbunsha, 1977.

Neustupny, J. V. *Gaikokujin to no Komyunikeishon* [Communicating with Foreigners]. Tokyo: Iwanami Shoten, 1982.

———. *Communicating with the Japanese*. Tokyo: Japan Times, 1987.

Otterbein, Keith F. *Comparative Cultural Analysis: An Introduction to Anthropology*. New York: Holt, Rinehart & Winston, 1977.

Redden, W. *Culture Shock Inventory Manual*. Atlanta: Measurement Systems Press, 1975.

Tanaka Mitsuo and H. Haarmann. *Yōroppa no Gengo* [The Languages of Europe]. Tokyo: Iwanami Shoten, 1985.

Index